The History of America

History Nerds

Published by History Nerds, 2021.

While every precaution has been taken in the preparation of this book, the publisher assumes no responsibility for errors or omissions, or for damages resulting from the use of the information contained herein.

THE HISTORY OF AMERICA

First edition. January 6, 2021.

Copyright © 2021 History Nerds.

ISBN: 979-8215121238

Written by History Nerds.

Also by History Nerds

Celtic History
Ireland

Great Wars of the World
World War 1
World War 2
The Napoleonic Wars: One Shot at Glory
The Serbian Revolution: 1804-1835
Peace Won by the Saber: The Crimean War, 1853-1856
The Wars of the Roses

Irish Heroes
Grace O'Malley: The Pirate Queen of Ireland
William Butler Yeats: Nobel Prize Winning Poet
Scáthach
Finn McCool

The History of the Vikings

Vikings
Longships on Restless Seas

The Rise and Fall of Empires
Rome: The Rise and Fall

Standalone
The History of the United Kingdom
The History of Ireland
The History of America
Stalin
The Fiery Maelstrom of Freedom
The History of Scotland
Robert the Bruce
William Wallace: Scotland's Great Freedom Fighter
The History of Wales

Table of Contents

Introduction

EXPLORERS FIRST CAME to America in search of spices. However, in the process of the search, they stumbled across a whole new unexplored continent.

Why did these people take the risk of sailing across an unfriendly sea to the raw, untried continent they discovered? Why were they willing to trade what they had – however mean or humble – for an unknown wilderness? They were creators in a sense. These Americans-to-be – men, women and children who wanted to take soil within their bare hands and mold it into the clay that would give rise to their vision for a future of their own making. Or was that journey just a figment from the collective imagination of leaders who wanted a family of people – mere, troubled actors to play the roles for the plays those leaders had written?

The United States was seen as a haven in which to form "a more perfect union, establish justice, insure domestic tranquility..." with the blessings of liberty. There was no room in America for dictators or kings. Again, the word "liberty" appears in the Declaration of Independence, one of the inaugural documents of America...liberty and the freedom to pursue the happiness each of its founders espouses.

Some of the earliest primary countries who ventured on to the unknown shores of America were from Spain, the Netherlands, France, Sweden and England. Reportedly there is historically accepted evidence that in the 10th century a Viking called Leif Eriksson set foot on North American soil.

The old world objectives of 'Conquer' and 'Conquest' didn't disappear in the United States for centuries. These new Americans brought with them some of the "Old-World" thinking. The search for liberty and freedom was fought by the United States over and over again throughout its history, on its own soil, and on the soil of other nations.

Was America a grand and glorious experiment in democracy? Was it a democratic Utopia? Or was it and is it a "work-in-progress?" It is up to the reader of this book to decide.

Chapter 1 – Is There a Better Way?

Sometimes Wrong, but Never in Doubt!

THE PALATES OF THE Europeans were tickled with the spices from Asia called the "Spice Islands." The "Spice Islands" lay in the southwestern Pacific Ocean and were obtained by traders for sale on the European market. Today, who would have dreamed that these spices – garlic, salt, cinnamon, ginger, turmeric, cardamon and pepper – were expensive? They were, in a sense, priceless. Without the benefit of refrigeration, they could be used to preserve meat and fish and had the added benefit that they could be used as flavorings and medicines.

That was, after all, the 15th Century.

Not only were there culinary items in the Far East, but flax, cotton and silk were prized for making textiles and clothing. Otherwise, the Europeans depended upon wool and furs.

Up until the year 1453, people used caravans of weary camels to transport those products overland via the Silk Road north of China. Then the great city of Constantinople fell to Sultan Mehmed II, leader of the Ottoman Turks. That great sultan boycotted trade with China. Travel through alternate routes meant that traders had to cross the deserts of the Near East, and were subject to attacks by robbers and kidnappers. Those who weren't killed were enslaved and disappeared.

An explorer by the name of Christopher Columbus read the *Travels of Marco Polo* and was lured by Polo's stories of these lands in China as well as the Spice Islands. Likewise, he, too, wanted to visit these markets and make a great deal of money to support himself and his family. He felt he would be rich and famous.

Christopher Columbus and one of his brothers, Bartolomeo, theorized that China could be reached by sailing west across the Atlantic Ocean. The Columbus brothers were both cartographers, and Christopher himself had studied the texts of Prince Henry the Navigator, a foremost nautical expert who had a school in Italy.

The maps at the time were fraught with inaccuracies in measurement. Columbus most likely used the *Imago Mundi*, which was a 15th Century map of the world. It was written by Pierre d'Ailly, a Catholic cardinal and scholar. D'Ailly had studied the work of an Arabian astronomer named Alfraganus and drew his map based on that information. What neither the good cardinal nor Columbus knew was the fact that there was a discrepancy between the Arab mile and the Roman mile used in Europe. Because of that error, historians estimated that Columbus calculated that the distance he would have to travel westward would be about 5,300 nautical miles. He was wrong! In reality, it's about 11,000 nautical miles – twice as far as he thought it would be! What would he tell his sailors if they found themselves in the middle of a wide blue ocean without the sight of land? Nevertheless, Columbus was a persuasive negotiator as well as a personable and skillful marketer.

Columbus had expertise in dealing with the wind at sea. As a very young man, he had sailed the Mediterranean sea. It was said that he worked at sea since age 10. In 1470, he worked for Rene of Anjou, a Duke, in his attempt to conquer the kingdom of Naples in Italy. After that, he moved to Lisbon, Portugal. Columbus worked for the wealthy Centurione, Di Negro and Spinola families making many voyages for them in their trading ventures. He is believed to have sailed as far north as Bristol, England and as far south as the Canary Islands, off the west coast of Africa even as a young man.

Personal Life

As the son of a humble wool weaver, Christopher was fortunate in marriage when he wed the lovely Filipa Moniz Perestrelo, a Portuguese noblewoman. Despite her elevated social station in life, she was a poor widow. Columbus had a big heart, as he demanded no dowry when they married in 1479 and made their home on the Portuguese Island of Porto Santo, not far from the Canary Islands. He and Filipa had one son, Diego.

When he returned from a trading assignment in Ghana, Africa, around 1484, he went home to Porto Santo, but discovered, much to his regret, that his wife had died. After that, he went to Portugal with Diego to settle her estate. On the way, it is said that he stopped at Cordoba in southern Spain where so many Genoese merchants used to gather. While there, he met a lovely 20-year-old woman by the name of Beatriz Enriquez de Arana, and they fell in love.

Quest for Financial Backing

While in Portugal, Columbus prepared up his ambitious proposal, along with his maps and cost projections for such a journey. Then he presented those plans to King John II of Portugal. The king passed along Columbus's projections to his own experts. Unfortunately, they rejected them.

Columbus wasn't a man easily discouraged, so he made arrangements to meet with King Ferdinand and Queen Isabella of Spain. Both of them were busy with their campaigns against the Moors at that time. Columbus told the court ministers about his mission, and they bid him to wait, which he so did. At their first opportunity, the court officials generally related the proposal to the Spanish Queen. She showed mild interest, and told Columbus she would let him know.

After Columbus left the court, he got word that Portugal's explorer, Bartholomew Dias, had just returned from a journey from Portugal to the Cape of Good Hope on the southernmost tip of Africa. Dias was attempting to show that a sea route to China and the Spice Islands would be feasible by going around Africa.

Now, Spain and Portugal were perennial rivals. So, when the Queen and her husband thought that the Portuguese might beat them to the Spice Islands and the wondrous markets of the East, they called upon Columbus. Columbus was, as a matter of fact, already on his way to France to present his proposal there when the Queen's messengers caught up with him and had him taken back to see the two regents. Their situation with the Moors was nearly resolved, so they gave his plans more attention.

Columbus was no fool, however. He knew human nature. To assure that he wouldn't be forgotten if he was successful, he indicated that he wanted to be officially named the "Admiral of the Ocean Sea," and wanted one-tenth of the profits from his discoveries! The royal couple was astounded at his boldness, but his offer was too tempting to reject. They wholeheartedly accepted it. They also indicated they would provide him with ships and gave him permission to press sailors into service.

Not So Fast!

The city of Palos in Spain owed the crown recompense for a past offense, and – in lieu of paying a large penalty – they were required to make vessels always available to the King and Queen upon request. Hence, ships were available or at least made available.

Columbus hand-picked some experienced seamen. He then selected three brothers from the well-known Pinzon family – Martin, Francisco and Vincente. He also took the three brothers with him. In addition, Columbus hired a physician and two barbers. To complete his complement of the major staff, he employed an assayer and a silversmith. Columbus was optimistically convinced he would find gold and silver in what he thought was China.

On August 3, 1492, Columbus headed out on three caravels with two to three masts each and massive sails. The ship called the *Santa Maria* was the largest. The other two – the *Nina* and the *Pinta* – were somewhat smaller. He planned on stopping at the Canary Islands first to pick up more supplies for the journey.

Before the ships could dock at the Canary Islands, there was an emergency. The *Pinta* floundered at Lanzarote Island, north of the Canaries. Her rudder was broken. In addition, the ship had been dry-docked too long and was in serious need of re-caulking.

Columbus tried to commission another ship, but none was available. Martin Pinzon, the captain, and his men jerry-rigged a substitute rudder and the *Pinta* limped into the harbor of Gran Canaria Island. Feverishly, the men worked on it, until it was seaworthy. While Columbus was there, he and his men saw a volcano starting to smoke and spew fire on Tenerife Island, just to the west of the Canary Island. It was time to go!

The Calm before the Storm

The crew set sail again on September 6, 1492. The ocean was deceptively smooth, unwrinkled by waves. Columbus saw that as a bad omen, and then it happened. Huge waves the size of "dragon's tongues" leaped up from the water and Columbus and the Pinzon brothers on their ships had the crew tack the sails to prevent being blown on their sides.

After the storm, Columbus realized they were headed toward the cold and treacherous North Atlantic. The three ships then corrected their course, to bear westward. After calm seas descended upon them, the sailors looked around them and saw nothing but the wide blue sea. Many shed tears and others panicked. Yet, Columbus was confident in his skills as a navigator and reassured them that they weren't that far from land.

Later historians noted from his logs that Columbus kept two sets of figures. He deliberately underestimated the number of leagues they'd traveled. A league is about 3/4 miles long. Cleverly, Columbus and used the fictional set of figures that to try to keep his sailors calm. To some extent, it worked.

Nature Intercedes

Toward mid-September, the seamen spotted a tern. Terns fly no further than six to eight miles away from land which gave the sailors the impression they may hit land soon. Columbus knew better, but permit them to take heart in that delusion.

Toward the end of September, booby gannets landed on the masts of the Pinta and delighted the sailors. They also saw floating herbs and seaweed. After the appearance of the flora and fauna, though, the seas became mysteriously quiet, but the waves rose and fell in great swells. The sailors had no time to fret, as they spent most of their days tacking the sails in order to catch what little wind there was. The men began to panic and begged Columbus to turn around and head back to Spain. When the winds picked up again, Columbus knew he had hit the trade winds, and his crews felt better. However, Columbus and the Pinzon brothers noted that the ships had traveled much further southwest than they had anticipated. According to his estimates, Columbus and the Pinzon's thought they should have reached land at that point, but hadn't. Carefully, they studied his logs and measurements and estimated that Columbus had gone nearly 2,200 nautical miles west of the Canary Islands. Their calculations were inaccurate as they had anticipated that the Atlantic Ocean was only 1,700 miles wide.

Flying fish were sighted, so Columbus and the Pinzon's thought they were close to Japan, which was then called "Cipango". Martin Pinzon, in particular, disagreed and became belligerent because it didn't match any of the descriptions. Arguments eventually erupted. They thought somehow they'd missed Japan and Columbus was to blame. Some even whispered words of mutiny.

Land Ahoy!

The sea grew eerily quiet, and everyone was apprehensive, until flocks of birds were sighted and even terns and ducks! Fresh green plants were also seen floating on the waves. That night, a call rang out. Land ahoy!

Columbus and the seamen scrambled to the deck. There, in the distance was a faint light flickering. In the morning of October 12, 1492, they landed. Historians indicate that their landing site was most likely Las Casas island in the Bahamas. Columbus, a religious man, named it "San Salvador," meaning "Holy Savior."

Chapter 2 – The "Indians"

WHEN PEOPLE CAME FORWARD from the trees on the island, Columbus and his men were astonished. The men had copper-colored skin and were naked. Their bodies were painted in white, black and red. In his journal, Columbus wrote, "They appeared to be a race of people very poor in everything. The go about naked as when their mothers bore them." Could these be the people who sent spices and silk to Europe? Then Columbus spotted gold earrings on some of the natives. Gold! Certainly Queen Isabella and King Ferdinand would be delighted. Columbus and his men left a few trinkets for the natives, and they shared gifts with him such as shells and colored stones. We now believe these people were members of the Lucayan, Taino and Arawak tribes.

Thinking he'd reached the Indies, Columbus named them "Indians," and asked where he might find more gold. An ambitious man came aboard his ship and led Columbus to a large heavily forested island with more natives. After dispatching a few sailors to explore, they returned without any gold. Columbus then had his men grab a few of the "Indians" and insisted that they lead him to the islands where gold could be found. He desperately wanted to return to Queen Isabella with treasures.

The Islands

Columbus and his crew sailed from island to island to explore. The people on most of the islands were friendly, though – but on one island – Columbus reported they "ran like hens." Columbus and his men explored what is today Plana Cays, Fortune Island, Long Island in the Bahamas, and then Haiti, the Dominican Republic, Hispaniola and Cuba, where he made several stops at large harbors, conducive to the landing of the large sailing ships the Europeans used in the 15th Century.

The Gold!

At one of his stops, he found small villages called *bohios*. The houses were well-built and had tall chimneys. Furniture was sparse, but there were beds made of netting. The islands were rich and fertile. He and his men gathered samples of the herbs they could find, none of which was recognizable. When he asked for pepper, the people were confused at first, but offered him chili pepper, which they called *api*. It grew wild on the islands. Columbus killed a snake on one island, and took its skin as a gift for the queen. There were many oysters near the shore which were found at short depths near the glittering beaches.

Sinking of the *Santa Maria*

On Christmas Day of 1492, the *Santa Maria* ran aground off the shores of Haiti. The ship had been badly damaged, so they cannibalized it for timber and removed what supplies they could. The people of the island came forth to help. That's when Columbus came across the gold. After seeing Columbus so cheered at the sight of gold the chieftain of the area awarded Columbus with a beautiful mask that had gold eyes and gold ornamentation on it. More of the natives brought small pieces of gold which they exchanged for trinkets.

Columbus was planning on his return voyage, but left behind some 39 men. They were charged to build a fortress there, explore the coast and search for gold The settlement was called La Navidad, after the birth of Jesus Christ. On January 10 of 1493, the *Nina* and *Pinta* set sail for the Azores, islands off the west coast of Africa.

Finally Home

On February 18, 1493, Columbus and his ships docked at the island of Santa Maria in the Azores, after being blown there by bad weather. The Azores were colonial possessions of the Portuguese, so

Columbus and his crew were interrogated by the governor of the island. Wisely, Columbus refused to let them board. His presentation of letters from the King and Queen of Spain made little difference, so Columbus assumed that Spain and Portugal weren't on good terms at that time. Eventually, though, King John II of Portugal called upon him to see him. Because of storms, they weren't able to meet until March 5th at the Vale do Paraiso hostel, north of Lisbon. They were properly greeted and feasted by the King.

Columbus also met Bartholomew Dias, the famed Portuguese explorer, who sailed around Africa and landed in the Far East. They exchanged stories and information. By then the news was out and crowds came out to greet the sailors and gape at the natives they'd brought with them. Trumpets blew, banners waved, and bands played on.

On March 15, 1493, Columbus and his men reached Spain and greeted King Ferdinand and Queen Isabella. They brought a few of the "Indian" people with them along with samples of gold nuggets, cotton, chili peppers, rhubarb, raw cinnamon and samples of plants. When he showed them the golden mask the chieftain in the islands had given him, the sovereigns were thrilled. He described the fertile fields, the pastures and the plains. They were somewhat disappointed though that there wasn't that much gold. However, Columbus told tales of the possibility of a wealth of gold mines and many more treasures if more of the lands could be explored.

The Race Was On!

When Amerigo Vespucci, an Italian explorer, returned from his voyage in 1499, he discovered that Columbus hadn't disembarked at the Indies. He wrote in a letter to Lorenzo Medici, a noted statesman from Florence, Italy, that he discovered the *Mundus Novus,* that is, a "New World!"

Only a few countries in Europe were knowledgeable in the building of these great clipper ships – the three-masted caravels and barques, the two-masted carracks, galleons, frigates, brigantines and the like. Those countries were Spain, England, the Netherlands and France. People came for a myriad of reasons – mercantilism, wealth, territory and religious freedom.

In the countries in Europe at that time, most countries had state religions. During the early Middle Ages, some people were persecuted because of their religion. To counteract the arrival of Protestantism, the Catholic Church conducted a shameful process known as the Inquisitions. Practitioners of those non-Catholic denominations were dragged in front of ecclesiastical courts and tried for heresy. Under the Spanish Inquisition alone, it was estimated that 32,000 people were either burned at the stake or stretched out on the rack until dead. The people of Great Britain, on the other hand, were required to join King Henry VIII's Church of England. Even so, a group of austere observers, the Puritans, were persecuted for insisting upon changes in practices in the Church of England. Those who didn't were persecuted. When the Catholic queen, Mary I, also known as "Bloody Mary," was on the throne in England, she executed hundreds of Protestants. In France, the Huguenot sect, even though it was Protestant, was deemed unacceptable and those people were sometimes massacred *en masse*.

Chapter 3 – Early Colonization

IN 1494, POPE ALEXANDER VI issued a bull leading to the Treaty of Tordesillas. That treaty divided the area in the new world via a north-south line. To the east of that line, Portugal was allowed to colonize, while Spain would colonize the lands west of there. There were only few lands that lay east of the line, so Portugal appealed to Pope Julius II to alter the line westward. He did so in 1506.

Astonished by this overreach of papal authority and the audacity of Spain and Portugal to make such a stipulation, most other countries ignored it.

Many of the initial attempts at colonization failed due to unforeseen hardships and challenges. The early settlers had little to no idea with regard to the fertility of the soil, nor the climactic conditions. Thus, many people starved. The new World also carried diseases unheard of in Europe. What's more, much of the land was already inhabited by tribes of indigenous Native Americans. Some clans were friendly, but others resented the intrusion of these strange foreigners upon their hunting grounds with their buildings and fences.

The Lost Colony of Roanoke

One of the most notable of the early colonial failures to establish a settlement was at Roanoke colony an island off in today's state of North Carolina. In 1585, an English explorer, Sir Walter Raleigh, was commissioned by Queen Elizabeth of England to establish a settlement there. Under the newly appointed governor, Ralph Lane, settlers landed on Roanoke Island. There, they met some of the local tribes, the Pamlico, the Aquasocogoc and the Secotans. They were friendly and helpful, and provided food for the settlers until they could establish flourishing farms. The Secotans often warned Lane about other hostile tribes that were warlike. To protect themselves, the settlers built a fort.

The new colonists noted that the natives used a great deal of copper, and asked them to lead them to the source of the copper. However, that entailed involvements with other native tribes. In the course of time, Lane became absorbed in various inter-tribal disputes and hostilities. Their relations with the Secotans soured. However, once they were able to re-establish good relations, other tribes reacted with negatively. Some of the native leaders were killed by hostile tribes. When the leader of the Secotans, Pemisapan, was slaughtered by another tribe, the English were vulnerable.

With the help of the Moratuc tribe, the English did explore parts of the mainland. However, Lane and his party depended upon food from the Moratuc for the journey, this however turned out to be an error. Several months later, Lane and his men returned to the colony empty-handed and half-starved, saying that they had discovered only abandoned villages and corpses of fallen natives.

The English settlement was awaiting more supplies from England,which were delayed in arriving. Finally, in 1586, Francis Drake did arrive, but Lane and the settlers decided to abandon the colony and sail back to England. Two weeks later, another ship arrived led by John White. It was now 1587, and it was White's responsibility to hold on to Raleigh's claim, so he re-established the Roanoke colony. He disembarked there and a settlement of approximately 120 people was created. While there, John White had a granddaughter born, Virginia Dare. She was the first English child born in America.

In 1588, White returned to England to bring back more supplies for the colony. While in Europe, White was delayed due to the Anglo-Spanish War. In 1590, White and his men finally arrived to find the settlement completely abandoned. The only possible clue that was found was the word "Croatoan," carved into the defensive wall around the colonists' houses. Investigations led later on by a neighboring colony, that of Jamestown, Virginia, yielded no answers. Various theories have been purported ever since, included a massacre by the natives or assimilation into one of their tribes. Archeologists have also conducted research in the area, but no evidence ever surfaced.

Other Failures

Roanoke wasn't the only disastrous attempt at colonization. Other attempts were made in the current-day states of Georgia (in 1526), three in Florida (1526, 1559, 1564), South Carolina (1562), North Carolina (1567), Virginia (1570), Texas (1685) and Maine (1607). Disease, starvation and killing by hostile natives were the most frequent causes of the failure to create permanent settlements.

New Mexico

Many of the initial settlements founded by Spain lay in Central America (Mesoamerica), islands in the Caribbean Sea, Mexico and South America. Between 1540 to 1542, Francisco Vasquez de Coronado and his party traveled north from Mexico to explore the deserts and open plains of today's state of New Mexico. He took hundreds of sheep, horses and mules with him. De Coronado envisioned that there was gold there, but left disappointed. In 1598, Juan de Onate also came north from Mexico with his soldiers and livestock. In addition, he had missionaries with him – the Franciscans. He established a more permanent settlement called "San Juan de los Caballeros," meaning Saint John of the Knights. They encountered the tribal people, the Pueblos, the Apaches, Navajos and Comanches. Onate remarked that people from those tribes lived in houses with terraces, much like the Spanish lived. It was Onate's desire to subjugate them however. In 1610, he founded the city of Sante Fe, which became the state capital in time.

Battles with the Natives

The colonists conducted raids upon the tribes, and exploited native labor for building and other chores, selling some into slavery. Even the priests were believes to abuse those native to the lands. They used them for erecting missions and even attempted to enforce baptism upon them.

In 1598, the Acoma Pueblo tribes revolted against the severe repression. As result of the battles, Juan de Onate lost 11 soldiers, but slaughtered hundreds of the Pueblos. Viciously, Onate punished all the males 25-year-olds and older by amputating their left feet.

In order to curry favor from the Spanish sovereigns, King Philip III and Queen Margaret, and entice them to continue to provide financial support, the Franciscans "baptized" 7,000 of the natives in 1608. At that time, Spain, a Catholic country, insisted that its colonists convert to Catholicism. The tribal people attended Mass, but secretly continued to practice their ancestral religion. During the 1650s, Governor Bernardo Lopez d Mendizabal and his associate, Nicolas de Aguilar forbid the priests to punish the Indians, and permit the native people to practice their own religions.

During the 1670s, a famine occurred due to a severe drought. When the tribal people came to beg food from their Spanish overlords, the Spanish couldn't help them, as they, too, were inflicted with the famine.

The Pueblo Rebellion

In 1680, under the leader of the Pueblos, Ohkay Owingeh, also called "Po'pay," they rebelled. The Pueblos killed 400 settlers, driving the remaining 2,000 of them out. Just prior to the rebellion, a subtribe of the natives, the Piro Pueblos, were allied with the Spanish. They, too, settled in El Paso with the Spanish.

Spanish Reconquest

Between 1692 and 1696, various attempts were made; treaties were made and broken, and made again between the Indians and the Spanish who trickled back to Sante Fe under Diego de Vargas. There was another Pueblo revolt in 1696. By the end of the 17th Century, the Pueblos were finally overcome. They were given land grants and a public defender was hired to protect their rights.

Saint Augustine, Florida

In 1560, King Philip of Spain appointed the conqueror, Pedro Menendez de Aviles, as the Captain General of the Spanish fleet, and his brother Bartolome Menendez as an admiral. That fleet explored the east "Indies," meaning the islands in the Caribbean. During that time, both Spain and France were in a race to claim Florida for their respective monarchs. In 1565, King Philip II of Spain commissioned Menendez to explore the area. At the end of August, he founded a settlement he called Saint Augustine, named after the saint on whose feast day he made landfall. St Augustine is the oldest continuously occupied settlement in the United States.

After that, the French fleet under Captain Jean Ribault headed toward Saint Augustine to oust the Spanish. Taking advantage of a wind squall that held back the French fleet, Menendez disembarked his troops and marched upon the French fort north of there – Fort Caroline. As the garrison was only lightly defended, Menendez overcame the French. He then killed most of the men, but spared the women and children. The men's bodies were hung in trees, with a sign reading "Hanged, not as Frenchmen, but as 'Lutherans.' They weren't even Lutherans, however. They were Huguenots – a splinter group formed from the Lutherans. In time, the word "Lutheran" stood for heretic.

The settlers at Saint Augustine made peaceful relations with the indigent tribes. In 1586, though, Sir Francis Drake, acting on behalf of the English, attacked the town and burned it. Menendez had seen their approach and the people were successfully evacuated. To retaliate, the Spanish sent out expeditions against the English colony at Jamestown, Virginia.

Jamestown, Virginia

Jamestown was the first permanent English colony in America. It was established in 1607 by the Virginia Company of London. First, they built a fort there for protection. There were Native Americans there – the Powhatan family of tribes. The Powhatans weren't friendly, and neither was the Paspaheigh tribe. Wars ensued between them and with the English settlers. In time, the English gained control, and ousted the natives.

Between 1609 and 1610, more than 80% of the settlers died from disease or starvation. For a short period of time, the English abandoned the colony due to the hardships. When resupply ships arrived, they settlers returned. In 1619, they shipped in slaves from a privately-hired Dutch ship. The people planned on setting up tobacco plantations and wanted these African slaves to work the fields.

<u>Bacon's Rebellion</u>

In 1676, the settlers rebelled against the governor who the English had appointed as head of the colony. That action was called Bacon's Rebellion. After the settlement was burned due to the fighting, the people moved their settlement to Williamsburg, Virginia in 1699. A sister colony was thereafter established at Yorktown. Williamsburg was eventually restored and reconstructed. Today, it is a famed historical site.

Massachusetts Bay Colony

In England, the mandatory religion was the Church of England, and there were specific observances expected of the followers. However, there was a group of people who disagreed with certain practices of the Church of England. They felt that the church was very lenient and too closely resembled the Roman Catholic religion. They called themselves the "Puritans." Those people were more austere in their beliefs and practices. The Church of England rejected them, and the Puritans sought refuge in America.

In 1621, they arrived on the shores of Plymouth Heights in Massachusetts and created a settlement there. The Native tribes there –

the Wampanoags and the Pokanokets along with others – were initially very welcoming, and even celebrated a feast with them to thank God for their arrival and for the food the natives shared. That feast became known as Thanksgiving and is a national holiday in America.

Wisely, they created a set of laws and provisions for the people of the settlement to follow. That document was called the Mayflower Compact, named after the flagship that carried the Pilgrims to the new land.

That colony gave rise to the creation of the Massachusetts Bay Colony that eventually expanded to include all of today's state of Massachusetts. They conducted a fruitful fur trade with the Native Americans, specifically the Narragansett tribe.

<u>The Salem Witch Trials</u>

The practice of "witchery" was strictly forbidden by the Puritans who had been victimized by the superstitions of times gone by. Many woman who used herbs were accused of witchcraft.

In the colony, a woman named Sara Good was accused of witchcraft after two other women – Abigail Williams and Elizabeth Parris – were said to have been bewitched by her. From the description of their behavior, it appears that they actually may have been epileptics. When asked by their preacher, Samuel Parris, "who torments you," they responded "Sara Good." Reverend Nicholas Noyes, who was the judge at her trial, listened to the story and the witnesses. He then sentenced her to be hanged. On July 19th, 1692, that took place. Noyes sentenced more women to the same fate. After several years, he became immersed in guilt and ceased acting as a judge. He was, however, succeeded by other judges, and they developed a formalized procedure for determining guilt. The witch trials continued until about twenty people were executed. In 1692, the governor of Massachusetts, Sir William Phipps, put an end to it.

New Sweden

Between 1621 to 1650, the New Sweden Company established nineteen settlements in the New World for their people and others from the Latvian states of Northern Europe, Norway, Russia, Poland and Germany. Those settlements were spread over today's states of Delaware, Maryland, Pennsylvania and New Jersey. Some of those settlements were lost to invasions by the English in 1655, with the exceptions of Swedesboro, New Jersey and Wilmington, Delaware. Swedesboro was annexed by the Dutch in 1655. Finns Point in New Jersey, was settled by the Finns in 1651 under Swedish sponsorship. That tiny settlement, along with its fort, Fort Casimir, was annexed by the Dutch, also in 1655. In 1664, it was overrun by the English.

Some areas in New Jersey still bear the names of the original Swedish settlers, like Sinnickson and Swedesboro.

New Netherland, New York-New Jersey-Delaware-Connecticut-Rhode Island

The Dutch didn't want to be left out of this new possible source of wealth and ownership of colonies in America. Around 1625, the Dutch West India Company widely explored the mid-Atlantic area of America. They then claimed a huge land area including territories in current-day states of New York, New Jersey, Massachusetts (Cape Cod), Delaware, and even part of Connecticut. They called this massive area "New Netherland."

One of their most important colonies was "New Amsterdam," that is, current-day Manhattan Island. It had deep-water ports and was ideal for trade. In 1626, Peter Minuet, representing the settlers, purchased it for the equivalent of $24 from the Native Americans. They also claimed "Lange Eylandt," today's equivalent of Long Island.

In 1633, the Dutch established a settlement at Hartford, Connecticut. Fort Hope was built there. Fort Nassau was built along the Hudson River in today's northern New York state near Albany. Another fort called "Roduins" was erected on the Housatonic River in Connecticut. Trade was set up between the settlers and the Lenni Lenape tribe who sold furs.

The Dutch engaged in a vigorous trade with the tribes, who trapped beavers for them. For beavers, the Dutch colonists traded axes, knives and wool. Hats made out of beaver pelts were extremely popular in England.

A Swedish colony had been established in current-day Delaware, but was abandoned until around 1655, the Dutch took it over. It was located at what is today the city of Wilmington.

The Dutch even laid claim to Rhode Island, which they then named "Roode Eylandt." The Narraganset tribes were very plentiful in the area and they had a good trade relationship. The Dutch established trading posts on the coast of New England and major tributaries as well.

A Puritan minister from Massachusetts named Roger Williams was expelled from the Massachusetts Bay Colony for religious differences with the Puritans. He moved his followers to Providence Plantations in Providence, Rhode Island after buying land from Wamsutta, the elder son of Massasoit of Wampanoag tribe. Unfortunately, that purchase wasn't negotiated between the Native Americans and the colonists. It was simply annexed. That triggered a war between those natives and the settlers in Massachusetts.

Williams founded the first Baptist Church in America. He also forbade slavery in his colony.

Not all of the settlers in New Netherland were Dutch. They welcomed other settlers, including Germans, Scandinavians, French Huguenots, Walloons – a minority group from Belgium – and some English who left the English settlements in the northeast.

The Dutch lived among the English settlers who migrated to New England and traded with them, as well as with the English settlers in and around Plymouth colony in Massachusetts.

The English and the Dutch fought three wars – the Anglo-Dutch Wars – in North and South America over control of colonies in the New World. The English, however, outnumbered the Dutch colonists in America. Due to England having an overwhelming force, Peter Stuyvesant, governor of New Amsterdam, realized that a mutually satisfying agreement could be reached with regard to the colony in America. Being that there were only 9,000 Dutch colonists spread out over the whole area of New Netherland and it could cause much unneeded bloodshed, Stuyvesant surrendered rights to its city, New Amsterdam, in 1664. That was followed up in 1673 by a trade-off arrangement between the Netherlands and England for the surrender of the remainder of New Netherland. In exchange, the Dutch were given the territory known as Suriname in South America.

New Netherland, including New York State, Long Island and Staten Island were then under English domination. In addition, New Jersey, Connecticut, Rhode Island, Delaware and Connecticut were included in that package.

Philadelphia and Pennsylvania

In 1681, William Penn, a wealthy Quaker from England was granted a charter by King Charles II of England. He then brought settlers into the great city of Philadelphia and today's state of Pennsylvania for religious refugees – his own Quakers – and also other dissenters – the Methodists and the Amish. Pennsylvania was a huge territory, and other Europeans took advantage of the western areas of Pennsylvania – the Scots, Irish and Germans.

Maryland Colony

In England at that time, Catholics were persecuted. So, in 1632, Maryland colony was established as a refuge for them. It was a proprietary colony founded by Cecil Calvert, known as Lord Baltimore. The city of Baltimore is named after him. This colony also tolerated Protestant dissenters as well. Maryland was the first colony to pass a Toleration Act, permitting full religious freedom for its inhabitants.

Province of Carolina

In 1670, this province was chartered by King Charles II of England to a group of English noblemen in exchange for their help in restoring him to the throne of England when he lost it to the upstart, Oliver Cromwel. Cromwell had overthrown the monarchy in England in 1653 during the reign of Charles II's father causing the English Civil War.

The Province of Carolina later spit into North and South Carolina.

Province of Georgia

Spain and England warred against each other for control of this southern territory just below South Carolina. In 1715, a war broke out between the British settlers of North and South Carolina, allied with the Cherokee and Carawba tribes against another Native American Federation – the Creeks, Yamasees and others. After the Carolinians gained control of the province, the Creeks and Yamasees fled. Much of the region was then depopulated, as some British settlers moved elsewhere.

In 1732, an English philanthropist and leader, James Oglethorpe, suggested to the English government that he could help alleviate the overcrowded prisons where debtors were sent. Oglethorpe obtained a charter and set up the Province of Georgia for the "worthy poor." The "worthy poor" were willing to work off their debts and became indentured servants. After an indentured servant paid off his debt, he was granted a plot of land to farm.

Province of Maine

The Province of Maine included the territories of current-day states of Maine, New Hampshire, Vermont and a portion of Massachusetts. In 1622, an open charter was granted by the kings of England for that area. In 1650, the Province of Maine was incorporated and granted to Ferdinando Gorges and John Mason, both Englishmen.

More Land Acquired

The French and Indian War, fought between 1754 to 1763, significantly reduced the area called New France. As result of that war, Britain gained all the property from the Atlantic Ocean to the Mississippi River. Certain areas of that land was designated as the "Indian Reserve." The remainder consisted of Florida and to the north, it included the Ohio River valley. Many of those lands hadn't yet been explored.

Chapter 4 – 17th Century America

CONFLICTS WITH NATIVE Americans

<u>The Anglo-Powhatan War 1610-1646</u>

In the tidewater section of Virginia and Southern Maryland, the Powhatan Tribal Confederacy under Chief Opechancanough arrived to greet the settlers of the territory with gifts of turkeys, fruit, fish and other foods. It was a ruse. Instead of freely giving the goods to the settlers, the natives snatched up their hatchets and knives and killed every person they could find. That included women and children. Blood gushed out of arteries; arms were hacked off and legs were gashed open. Bloodied body parts were strewn all over the settlement, and family dogs rushed into the woods howling. Approximately three hundred and forty seven people died.

The founder of the settlement, John Smith, was horrified, but was determined not to abandon his own settlement of Jamestown, Virginia. He then gathered up whom he could from the survivors of the Anglo-Powhatan War, along with more men in the smaller settlements of Southern Maryland then attacked the Indians in retribution. With maddened fury, they burned the native villages and their corn fields. The colonists pursued the Powhatans from place to place. For years, they fought each other. In 1644, 500 more colonists were killed. The settlers never gave up. As the native chief aged, he became ill and died in 1646. Having no vigorous and angry leader to continue the resistance, the Powhatan tribes retreated.

<u>The Pequot War 1636-1638</u>

Control of the fur trade heightened tensions between the Pequot tribe, the Mohegan tribe, and the Dutch and English colonists because profits were shrinking due to the competition. The triggering incident that ignited these growing tensions was the murder of a colonist, John Stone and his crew who arrived in a ship to receive furs. That was followed up by the murder of a Pequot sachem (leader). It accelerated when the Narragansett tribe became involved and a Puritan trader was killed.

The colonists of the Massachusetts Bay Colony, Plymouth Colony (Plymouth Plantations) in Massachusetts, the Connecticut Colony and their tribal allies, the Narragansett and Mohegan tribes waged a war. As result of this war along with 700 Pequots dying they also lost the war. Hundreds of the surviving Pequots were sold into slavery, and the remaining joined up with other tribes. As a tribe, the Pequots ceased to exist.

<u>Kieft's War 1643-1645</u>

This was a conflict set off because of the aberrant behavior of Willem Kieft, the first Dutch director of the Colony of New Netherland. He countermanded the wishes of the colonists by demanding tributary payments from the tribes who lived in the area and conducted trade. That was followed up by a series of reprisals including murders of colonists. Villages were raided by colonists and that accelerated into mutual massacres. As result, many Dutch settlers left the New World, and Kieft was replaced.

<u>King Philip's War 1675-1678</u>

This was one of the greatest wars ever fought between the early colonists and the Native Americans. It negatively affected future relationships with the Native American population in the Northeast. In the beginning, the Wampanoag chief, Massasiot, maintained a cordial relationship with the Puritans of New England when they first arrived in Massachusetts, but that changed in time.

When these two groups became enemies, it became necessary to set up boundaries between territories belonging to the natives and those belonging to the colonists.

It started in 1675, when the chief's younger son and successor, Metacom who called himself "King Philip," met up with Roger Williams who was trying to establish a colony in Plymouth Plantations. Plymouth Plantations lay just to the west of the Puritan settlements. The colonists considered William's settlement to be a violation of an agreement between the Puritans and the Wampanoag Tribe. The Puritans objected to the presence of Roger William's people because they weren't committed to Puritan ideals. That made them suspicious and Governor Josiah Winslow even jailed the tribal agent, Wamsutta, who had made the original arrangements for the sale. After the death of Wamsutta in 1663, Metacom/King Philip ruminated about this alleged offense. He then stirred up the neighboring members of Algonquin and Mohegan tribes in order to persuade them to assist in the pending hostilities. However, a tribal member, Wussausmon aka John Sassamon, who converted to Christianity, told the officials in Massachusetts about this pending war. Suddenly, John Sassamon was found dead of unknown causes.

Due to that incident, the Massachusetts officials arrested three Wampanoag natives. These tribal defendants were convicted and executed. Then the war really did break out which involved the colonists in New England allying with the Algonquins and Mohegans. Against that alliance, more tribes became involved including the Wampanoags, the Nipmucks, the Wabanakis and others.

This war was one of the largest between the early colonists and the tribal peoples. Twelve of the colonial towns were destroyed and the populations of both sides decreased significantly.

Economy

In New England, settlers wasted no time in building their settlements. They cut down trees and built dwellings for themselves equipped with fireplaces. The soil was poor, except for certain areas around rivers and water sources. Most New Englanders who lived near the coast were whalers and fishermen. Colonists used whale oil for making soap and candles. In the 18th Century, whales came relatively close to the shores, making capture convenient, but no less dangerous. They also conducted a brisk trade in furs, turpentine, grain, lumber and exchanged those products in the West Indies for sugar and molasses to make rum. The colonists exchanged their products with England for manufactured products like cloth, porcelain and the like. The area also gave rise to skilled tradesmen who made furniture, shoes and some clothing like beaver hats, ironware, tools and even pewter.

Initially, the basic economy was sustained by agriculture. The soil was richer in the middle states and down South. They grew wheat, millet and raised apple trees both for the fruit and apple cider, which was very popular. Livestock was raised with milk from the cows and eggs from chickens making up part of the colonists diet.

Once sheep were imported, the manufacture of woolen clothing grew. There were more villages and towns in the middle colonies, so that colonists could assist one another at times of need. The English writer and statesman, Edmund Burke, wrote in 1775, "The colonists have prosecuted agriculture in such a spirit that, besides feeding plentifully their own growing multitude, their annual export of grain has come for years exceeded a million pounds in value."

From the Southern plantations of Virginia and South Carolina came exports of tobacco and rice. Many of the larger plantations had African slaves, but smaller plantations and farms didn't have any, and were worked on by the farmer, his wife and children.

One of the most highly desirable products was one of the smallest – nails. Bog iron was accessible in the swampy areas. It formed over many years from peat. It was impure, of course, but could be collected in places like Batsto, New Jersey or Lake Massapoag in Massachusetts. The iron rocks were carried to those who created nail rods first, and then heated in large Forge Barns and cut them down to size. The first iron mines created were the Falling Creek Ironworks in Virginia built in 1619 and the Saugus Iron Works in Massachusetts in 1688.

Once they had nails, they built bridges over rivers and streams and wagons. Iron was also used to make farming implements like plows and hoes.

Taverns

Other than congenial gatherings for drinking alcoholic beverages, taverns served many other vital functions. They were originally called "ordinaries" or "Public Houses." They were gathering places for the colonists to discuss politics, product prices, issues related to farming, general sale of limited products, courtrooms, meeting and party rooms, post offices and religious meetings. As so many people had a need to travel, most taverns also served as hotels. The "Indian King" was one of the oldest taverns in Philadelphia. In order to attract customers, a Boston hatter opened a new tavern in 1770, and called it "The Hat and Helmet." He advertised that he would provide not only neighborly congeniality, but gave everyone a free newspaper.

Newspapers

Newspapers proliferated throughout the colonies. They were loaded with news and plenty of advertisements and announcements. In the *Virginia Gazette,* in 1770, it announced "A Match of Cocks," saying there was to be a cock fight between 25 cocks from a gentleman in Charles City and another in Sussex ... after which "there will be a ball and a reception for Ladies and Gentlemen." Announcements of importance also appeared, such as the arrival of a governor in 1771: "Yesterday arrived in town between ten and eleven o'clock, the Right Honorable the Earl of Dunmore, our governor...His lordship came through the Jerseys and Philadelphia and along the Eastern Shores of Maryland to this colony."

The newspapers were rife with editorials criticizing the hard-hearted manner in which these people were treated by the English.

Colonial Governments

Each one of the thirteen colonies had a governor appointed by England. The colonists had elective assemblies, which had jurisdiction over domestic matters. Even so, the governors had veto power over colonial legislation. That aroused the anger of the colonists, as they were considered English citizens and had no rights to vote on legislation passed that affected them and their livelihoods. British soldiers were posted in the large cities to collect taxes – a grim reminder that the British were their overlords.

Acts of Oppression

In 1651, England passed the first of many Navigation Acts. These forbade America from trading with countries other than England. That was an effort to restrict trade from America to its foreign rivals, Spain and France. England had been charging excise taxes as it was, but when the amounts became unreasonable, some American merchants resorted to smuggling. The British build custom houses to collect taxes at the ports. Despite all English efforts to curtail that. Americans found loopholes in the law and it continued.

Hostilities fomented among the colonists. Customs officers who arrived from England were often tarred and feathered. Some custom houses in Boston were vandalized as were their homes. When an English soldier guarding a custom house was threatened by a club-toting mob of angry settlers, he called for back-up. The English soldiers fired into the crowd, killing five colonists and wounding six others.

The Boston Massacre

Fights between colonists and English officials continually broke out, especially in Boston. Despite that, other colonists felt that these complaints were unjustified and treasonous. They sided with England in the disputes. These people were called Loyalists. The majority of Colonists felt otherwise, and craved for freedom from England. Riots and fights were common in the streets.

On a frigid day in March of 1770, a riot broke out between a group of colonists, armed with clubs, and a British soldier who was guarding a British custom house. Captain John Prescott arrived on the scene with a few soldiers to defend the establishment. The riot escalated and shots were fired. The crowd scattered, but there on the street lay the broken bloodied bodies of colonists – Crispus Attucks, Samuel Gray, and James Caldwell.

More Taxes!

In 1733, England passed the Molasses Act, charging a tax on molasses. Molasses was used not only as a sweetener, but to make rum. Then the Americans claimed they secured the molasses from Bermuda, a British colony, making it legal. Of course, Americans could also import it from islands in the Caribbean, which they so did.

In 1765, Great Britain passed the Stamp Act. Heated discussions erupted in the taverns throughout colonial America. The act required that paper imported from England have taxes levied upon it. The payment of that tax was confirmed by a special embossed seal. The Americans didn't have the skill to make their own paper, so they resorted to writing on the pages of old books and even the bark of trees. Of course, any legal documents had to have that special seal.

In 1767, the Townsend Acts were passed. They stipulated that:

- Americans must allow British soldiers to board in their homes, they must also feed and supply them as well
- Taxes were imposed on lead, glass and painters' colors. As America hadn't yet invented pigments, or found sources of lead, or had glass for their windows, this tax was a hardship
- This facet of the Townsend Acts provided for customs offices for British tax officials, mostly located at ports, to check that

taxes were paid on items shipped in

- In 1768, a codicil was passed that required that those accused of smuggling be hauled into court in England or tried by English judges in a special Vice-Admiralty Court.

The Tea Act of 1773 reduced the tax on tea, the most popular beverage in America. Because the British knew that the Americans were regularly smuggling in tea from the Netherlands, the act would encourage Americans to buy the tea from England which had originated from the British East Indies Company. The British East Indies company was on the verge of bankruptcy, and this was a means by which England might rescue them.

The Boston Tea Party

In 1773, a rebel organization, the Sons of Liberty, disguised themselves as Native Americans, boarded an English ship in Boston Harbor carrying tea and dumped as many as 343 chests of tea into Boston Harbor. Many British officers had never seen American tribesmen before, and were frightened. They were also startled by this flagrant act of disobedience and didn't intervene.

British Retribution

To penalize the colonists England passed a new series of acts in 1774 called the Coercive Acts. By virtue of those acts England entirely closed the port of Boston until such time that America would compensate Britain for the tea. Furthermore, it forbade the colonists from holding any public meetings and held all British officials immune from prosecution. The colonists sarcastically called those acts "The Intolerable Acts."

These colonists had taken a raw hard land and created not only colonies, but a whole new civilization. Their British overlords had taken more from them than they were entitled to. The settlers had no freedom to sell and buy from whom they pleased. They were English citizens themselves – intelligent and learned. What they didn't know by way of skills, they learned without teachers. The British soldiers on their soil, who ate of the food, who were taken care of within their hand-built homes treated them with disdain. They charged the Americans high taxes in order to pay for their own European wars. They colonists were furious.

After getting word about the blockade in Boston, a famous landowner (and future president) in Virginia, George Washington, called a general meeting (despite the ban). At that meeting, he leaped up and proclaimed, "I will raise a thousand men, subsist them at my own expense, and march them to the relief of Boston."

The First Continental Congress

In September of 1774, the colonists met in Philadelphia. Each of the thirteen original colonies was represented, although the one from Georgia was missing. The Georgians were engaged in a skirmish with some Native Americans at that time.

During the meeting, the clamor rose for independence. George Washington was there. So was Samuel Adams, a son of liberty member, and his brother, John Hancock, the learned lawyer and scholar, Peyton Randolph, a planter from Virginia, and Patrick Henry, a young and fiery orator. "The distinctions between Virginians, Pennsylvanians, Jew Englanders, Nee Yorkers are no more. I am not a Virginian," Patrick Henry called out, "I am an American!"

In an effort to stave off war and bloodshed, John Adams, a studious lawyer (and a future president), created a "List of Grievances" and sent it out to England. As a matter of fact, that list was never read by the King. Great Britain dismissed the colonists' complaints as an affront.

Battles of Lexington and Concord

Under the leadership of George Washington, the colonies decided to elect representatives who would discuss how to deal with the situation. They collected in a meeting house in Philadelphia in September of 1774.

In Boston, the British General, Thomas Gage, was well aware of the growing hostilities, and dispatched soldiers to march inland to empty the community arsenals of weapons.

Paul Revere and William Dawes, members of the Sons of Liberty, stood watch at Boston Harbor under the cloak of night to warn the Massachusetts colonists of the arrival of British soldiers. On April 18, 1775, Revere saw soldiers disembark from the British warship, HMS Somerset. Then they noted that the soldiers were taking the "water route," and hung two lanterns in the steeple of North Church, which was their pre-arranged signal. Revere, Dawes and other riders then galloped through the city and spread the warning.

As the British soldiers, whom they called "redcoats," marched through Lexington, the colonists kept steady watch on them from behind bushes and stone walls. As the British turned to march toward Concord they moved on to the "Green," a common area in the town. A shot rang out. According to Henry Wadsworth Longfellow's famous poem, it was the "shot heard 'round the world." To this day, no one knows who shot first, but the American Revolution had started.

Chapter 5 – The American Revolution

THE BATTLE OF "BUNKER Hill"

Actually fought at Breed's Hill on June 17, 1775, this was the site of an encounter with the British under Thomas Gage and a group of colonists armed with muskets. The Americans had insufficient gunpowder, but fought bravely. The British raced up the hill after them, and managed to capture the hill. Dead and dying men littered the hillside.

The Second Continental Congress

It seemed that the organizational meetings of the Continental Congress lagged behind the action. The sessions opened on July 2, 1775. One of their first actions was to make a last-ditch effort to avoid a full-scale war, so the delegates sent the "Olive Branch Petition" to Great Britain. It was carefully written and essentially asked that the king heed their requests for certain rights, one of which was to have their own representation in the English Parliament.

In case that was met with unsatisfactory results, the members spent days helping draft the *Declaration of Independence*. Thomas Jefferson, a statesman from Virginia was an excellent writer and was elected to write it.

George Washington, as a matter of fact, arrived at this meeting fully dressed in the uniform he wore when he had fought in the French and Indian War. He was known for his military skills, and was quickly chosen to be Commander-in-Chief if the war erupted.

King George III responded by declaring that America was in a state of rebellion.

Battle of Long Island

In July of 1776, General Washington had about 10,000 colonial recruits. He positioned some in forts along the Hudson River, and Governor's Island right in the heart of the harbor. Most of those forts were only partially constructed. He also had some unused ships towed into the harbor to prevent English warships from entering.

Washington then placed some colonials at Fort Washington and along the northern part of the Hudson River, today located at Washington Heights, New York. On the opposite side of the river, Fort Constitution was erected. At the tip of Manhattan, Washington placed cannons along with units of colonial soldiers most of which were poorly equipped and untrained. English ships arrived at New York Harbor. Some soldiers disembarked along the Hudson River at the American forts there. Many soldiers disembarked on Staten Island between New York and New Jersey. General William Howe of the British regiments marched into Brooklyn Heights on Long Island, New York and Manhattan Island with a twenty thousand soldiers in all. Howe placed his men in various strategic positions on the rocky hills located close to the city overlooking the East River. The colonists who lived in the area were threatened with harsh punishment if they were found informing Washington of British soldiers whereabouts.

English war ships continued to arrive and totalled forty five in the harbor. General Howe knew that the colonial soldiers weren't any match for the well-trained English regiments so he tried to play hero by sending messengers to make a "deal" with Washington. Three times he sent them and three times Washington sent them away. A meeting with Howe's adjutant was then scheduled. On behalf of the British, Washington was offered pardons. Loudly, Washington replied, "Those who have committed no fault want no pardon."

On August 22nd, the British Generals Henry Clinton and Charles Cornwallis left Staten Island and attacked Brooklyn. The British attempted to scale the rocks, but were picked off by colonial fire.

However, a colonial loyalist informed the British about a hidden pass up the steep slope to which they prepared to make a night attack. Their assault succeeded swarming over the whole area, shooting the colonials whose positions had been exposed whilst also taking a number captive.

It was now August 28th. At the area of Flatbush on Long Island, heavy fighting commenced between the colonials and the Hessians, who were German mercenaries in the employ of England. Heavy casualties mounted, and the Americans' left flank was left open. The British rushed in and hand-to-hand fighting was engaged. Some of the colonials surrendered, but they were immediately bayoneted by the Hessian soldiers. General John Sullivan signaled for the colonials in Flatbush to retreat.

In Manhattan, Washington's men bombarded the British with cannon fire, gunfire and artillery right into the night. As he surveyed the situation, Washington realized that the Americans were losing badly. He left a force of Pennsylvanians under Thomas Mifflin there shooting heavy musket fire to give the illusion that there were more colonials elsewhere. While it was dark, Washington planned a clandestine retreat to avoid any more bloodshed. The colonials slipped away in small boats in retreat. They then regathered in New Jersey and marched to Pennsylvania.

The British then moved in and occupied New York.

The American Double Agent

Washington and his troops traveled a long march in the cold and snow along the eastern border of Pennsylvania, doggedly followed by General Charles Cornwallis at a safe distance. Washington was surprised when he was approached by a man named John Honeyman from Griggstown, New Jersey. Washington had met him briefly at the Continental Congress. He volunteered to act as a double agent, and bring Washington information on the whereabouts of the British troops. Honeyman let on to the Loyalists among the colonials that he favored Britain and discovered that the Hessians planned to celebrate Christmas at a loyalist's house in Trenton.

Battle of Trenton and Battle of Princeton

Stealthily, Honeyman sailed back across the Delaware River at night and headed straight for Washington, giving him this vital information. On the night of December 25, 1776 – Christmas – Washington and his troops quietly sailed across the river toward Trenton. Washington separated his troops – one under Nathaniel Greene and John Sullivan. They were told to set up an encampment in Princeton nearby, but hide in the woods and leave their campfires burning to deceive the enemy into thinking the colonials were all encamped there. Washington and Henry Knox with their cannons also sailed across and set the big guns in place facing a garrison in Trenton where the Hessians were having their Christmas celebration. They let loose the cannons at the garrison, but the Hessian Colonel Johann Rall only had enough time to rally half of his men. He himself was shot off his horse and killed.

The Collapse of British Strategy

In New York State, the British had planned on sending General St. Leger along the St. Lawrence River and then south to Albany in upstate New York. General John Burgoyne was supposed to rally his troops and march by Lake Champlain and then south to Albany. General Howe was planning on coming north from New York and also up to Albany. That would effectively cut off the northern colonies from the rest.

However, General Howe disobeyed orders because he saw an opportunity to attack Philadelphia first. When Howe didn't show up as was planned, General St. Leger's British soldiers and also his tribal mercenaries were roundly defeated by American frontiersmen. That left only General Howe at Albany. The New Englanders were now free to come down south with supplies and help in the war effort.

Howe traveled up the Chesapeake Bay, and met up with Washington at Brandywine Valley in Pennsylvania. Unfortunately,

Washington lost the Battle at Brandywine. He tried again at Germantown, but lost there as well.

Howe moved into Philadelphia with his Biriths forces and occupied the city causing members of the Continental Congress to flee.

Battle of Saratoga

Burgoyne had tried to reach Albany, as he was supposed to do, but Leger had fled to Canada. Fighters from New England descended upon the area, felling trees in order to slow down Burgoyne's advance. Burgoyne then turned south, hoping to meet up with St. Leger or Howe. With Leger in Canada and Howe trapped in Philadelphia, Burgoyne was on his own and his supplies were running short.

Militiamen and colonials from New England and New York under General Horatio Gates formed up battle groups and went after Burgoyne. On October 17, 1777, Burgoyne reached Saratoga. There he and his troops faced nearly 20,000 Americans. After a bloody battle, Burgoyne surrendered.

Troop Movements

The impressive win at Saratoga convinced France to become allies with America. As the Americans had no navy of their own, France's aid became a tremendous help. The Marquis de Lafayette, a renowned military man in France had been following the fight for American Freedom. He leaped at the chance to help out the Americans and financed his own journey across the ocean to join General Washington.

The English had replaced the disobedient General Howe with Sir Henry Clinton who saw the occupation of Philadelphia as a waste of strength. He tried to ascertain the placement of Washington's largest forces, while watching the French at the same time. Clinton then decided to go back into New York on the chance Washington would have moved back there to expel the English from the port.

During the brutal winter of 1777 to 1778, Washington and his troops wintered at Valley Forge, New York. The Marquis de Lafayette was there as was the Baron von Steuben, a former Prussian military officer. To help the troops stay warm and to help them ready themselves for the rest of the fight, they trained the soldiers vigorously. It was a hard winter. Some died and others became ill.

The Franco-American Alliance

In 1780, France signed an agreement to help America in its war efforts. They sent Jean-Baptiste Donatien comte de Rochambeau and 7,000 French soldiers along with a fleet of ships to help.

When the weather lifted, the British Commander, Archibald Campbell, attacked and captured Savannah, Georgia. He was joined by Brigadier General Augustine Prevost who marched his troops from St, Augustine, Florida capturing American posts along the way. He also took control of Augusta, Georgia.

Rochambeau, Washington and Lafayette discussed their strategy. They could either move north and free up New York, or move south and retake Savannah. When Lafayette indicated that the French had additional ships headed up by Admiral de Grasse in the West Indies who could come north briefly to corner the British at a Southern port, Washington was delighted and they agreed to embark on that strategy.

While Washington and Rochambeau were *en route*, Sir Henry Clinton was on his way from from New York and placed a siege upon the port of Charleston, South Carolina. In May of 1780, General Benjamin Lincoln was forced to surrender the garrison there. However, the British didn't know whether Washington was going to stage his major attack in New York or down South, therefore, Clinton returned to New York.

Washington left some troops in New York to protect the Hudson Valley and confuse the English as to his plans. He did that as part of a ruse to confuse the enemy as to where the bulk of American forces would attack. Then Rochambeau, Lafayette and Washington led the American forces on a very long march – 460 miles! – from New Jersey and down south.

It was now 1981 and the British commander, George Cornwallis was in North Carolina. While there, smaller Patriot forces kept beating the English in battles such as the Battle of Kings Mountain, the Battle of Cowpens and the Battle of Cowan's Ford. General Nathaniel Greene was excellent at stirring up skirmishes like that, which turned the war in America's favor. Little by little, Greene's men killed off a number of the British who were reconnoitering in the South. As he was losing troops, Cornwallis attempted to gain Loyalists' support in North Carolina, but utterly failed. As he had lost so many men to Nathaniel Greene in the smaller battles, he sent word to Clinton in New York to send reinforcements. Cornwallis also had many men down, stricken with malaria. Frustrated with his lack of progress due to the sickness, General Charles Cornwallis took it upon himself to leave the Carolinas and shifted his base of operations to Virginia.

Once Washington, Rochambeau and Lafayette reached Virginia, Lafayette was sent out with a smaller contingent to confront the approaching troops under Cornwallis and keep him busy near Richmond. Lafayette was joined by the Virginia militia and sent out smaller vanguard squads to pretend to forage for food to feed the men. That was an attempt to deceive Cornwallis into believing that there were many more troops behind.

Soon afterwards, Cornwallis abandoned the Lafayette offensive and headed toward Yorktown. He had his soldiers build redoubts and fortifications near entrances to Yorktown. He then abandoned some to move the bulk of his forces closer to the north.

Washington and Rochambeau marched out of Williamsburg and descended into the grounds around Yorktown. Immediately, he had his troops build a series of redoubts to keep the British out of Yorktown. They found the abandoned British redoubts and used them. In addition, the men build trenches and more redoubts all over the outskirts of Yorktown to slow Cornwallis's advance.

At sea, Admiral de Grasse sailed up from the West Indies and blocked the harbor at Yorktown to prevent British vessels from entering. Admiral Graves finally arrived with the British ships, and exchanged shots.

Gunfire and the blast of artillery shells erupted from everywhere in the Yorktown area. The Americans then tore apart the British forces. The air filled with smoke and the pounding of artillery was thunderous. The Americans and French fired volley after volley at the British who returned fire. The Americans charged the British redoubts and fought them hand to hand. Blood flew in every direction as the soldiers bayoneted them to death. The British fire was heavy, but in the end the Americans overcame them. Washington surrounded Yorktown by three sides and kept firing at the British so they couldn't enter the port area. The gunfire intensified, until Cornwallis attempted to evacuate his troops across the York River just to the north where some of his troops were waiting. As if fate had dealt him a bad hand, a squall blew over the river, making it impossible for Cornwallis to cross.

In the morning of October 17, 1781, Cornwallis surrendered.

The Peace of Paris and the Treaty of Versailles

In September of 1783, King George III of England signed the Peace of Paris, granting independence to the United States and give up all rights to the Thirteen Colonies. The Treaty of Versailles was signed by Charles Gravier, the foreign minister representing King Louis XVI of France. This was the end of British North America.

Chapter 6 – The Federalist Period

GEORGE WASHINGTON, hero of the American Revolution, became America's first president. In 1781, the *Article of Confederation* were written. However, America – having been subjected to a monarchical form of government – wrote that document in such a way that the central government had very little power. It was more like a federation of friendship than a law of the land. States were in rivalry with each other over commerce and taxes. Resentment grew. What's more, there was no national currency recognized by other countries and that caused problems with foreign merchants. In addition, that caused problems because there was no national treasury with which to pay for government or the military.

The U.S. Constitution

Leaders of the Continental Congress and the military had made a name for themselves, and a series of meetings were held in Annapolis, Maryland. That assembly was called the Constitutional Convention. They had to act quickly, but thoughtfully, in order to keep the union together and draw up a set of laws.

James Madison was a brilliant young man of 25. He wasn't physically a strong man, however. When he enlisted in the Virginia Militia to serve in the American Revolution, he fainted on the first day he was supposed to report for duty! After recovering, he did train with the other men, but wasn't fit enough for the rigors of war, although it should be said he was an excellent marksman. Shortly afterward, he was drummed out of the military, but his fellow soldiers encouraged him to go into politics. Madison sincerely wanted to make his contribution.

People from Virginia, who knew of his intelligence and organizational skills, elected him to the Constitutional Convention.

Most of the elected representatives were busy at home, repairing their homes after the war and taking care of their farms and businesses after so much neglect. Madison then made it his responsibility to keep members from abandoning the effort. His organizational skills held the effort together, and he was able to demand participation. William Pierce, who had served in the war, said of Madison that "every person seems to acknowledge his greatness. In the management of every great question he took the lead and...always came forward as the best informed man of any point in the debate. James Madison became known as the "Father of the Constitution."

The final ratification of the U.S. Constitution took place in 1789. It provided for three branches of government – the Executive, the Legislative and the Judicial. To that, the Bill of Rights was added, guaranteeing specific rights to every American citizen. The various states wrote their own state constitutions, as each state had differing needs in certain areas like farming in the south and manufacturing in the north.

President Washington had a personally-selected set of men who handled different aspects of the administration: Secretary of State Thomas Jefferson; Secretary of the Treasury Alexander Hamilton; Secretary of War Henry Knox; and Attorney General Edmund Randolph.

Political Parties

Within Washington's cabinet, there were arguments between Alexander Hamilton and Thomas Jefferson. When Hamilton proposed a Federal Bank, Jefferson vehemently objected. Hamilton felt that the central government could interpret the Constitution loosely and shouldn't only be limited to what was specifically listed in the Constitution. They were called "loose constructionists." He further felt that the "well-born" should be given more power to pass decrees, but Jefferson had greater faith in the common people and was a firm believer in states' rights.. Hamilton was in favor of levying a tariff on foreign products so as to increase opportunities for American manufacturers to make headway in the world. Jefferson, though objected to that, as he wanted America to be a nation of farmers, and the benefit given to the manufacturers wasn't fair, as the farmers couldn't have such a benefit. He personally felt that there would be a rise of urban elite in the Northeast. He wanted to see more freedom given to the individual to regulate his own pursuit of industry especially on the local level.

Two parties emerged – the Federalist Party and the Democratic-Republicans. The Federalists favored a strong federal government, while the Democratic-Republicans favored more power for the states.

John Adams

John Adams followed Washington into the presidency, but walked into difficulties with foreign relations. There were unresolved issues after the Peace of Paris at the end of the American Revolution. First of all, the British had forts on American soil and were resistant to dismantling them. The Americans weren't forceful on that point during Washington's administration because Great Britain was still its greatest trading partner. In 1793, war between England and France and other European counties broke out because of the French Revolution. England then started seizing Americans from their ships and pressing them into service. What's more, America was shipping goods and war materials to Britain, and its enemy, France, objected. Therefore, France started seizing American ships. By 1797, they had 300 of them.

Adams sent John Marshall, Elbridge Gerry and CC Pinckney to France to settle the matter. Three secret French agents called "X," "Y" and "Z," met with them. Those three agents promised to stop confiscating American ships if America paid them a sum of $250,000, and if Adams would make an apology to France for uttering a negative statement to his Congress about them, and, in addition, extend a loan of $12 million to help France pay off their war debt! It was – in essence- a bribe.

America turned that offer down. The Convention of 1800 was passed in its stead, which did resolve the issue, although not to everyone's satisfaction. Adams was in favor of it because he wanted to avoid yet another war but America wouldn't have been able to afford it.

Alien and Sedition Acts

Ostensibly, to protect people from the infiltration of French agents into America, Adams proposed the Alien and Sedition Acts to Congress in 1798. However, he also used that law to eliminate the threat of Americans criticizing his behavior. He had newspaper editors arrested and convicted of sedition against America. One target of those laws was the grandson of the famous statesman and inventor, Benjamin Franklin. In his newspaper, the young man wrote described the president as "old, querulous, bald, blind, crippled, and toothless." Benjamin Franklin Bache, among a number of others, were prosecuted under those acts.

The Democratic-Republican Party voters became alarmed about the Alien and Sedition Laws, saying that those acts broke the First Amendment. The acts were then repealed during the presidency of Thomas Jefferson who succeeded Adams. Jefferson was a Democratic-Republican. One aspect was rewritten as the Alien Enemies Act that covered treason.

The Louisiana Purchase

Perhaps the greatest accomplishment of the Jefferson administration was the Louisiana Purchase. When Jefferson took office, Napoleon of France owned a huge chunk of land in the center of the United States. American farmers in particular craved that land, which is still called the nation's "breadbasket." Surmising that Napoleon was running out of funds to finance the spread of the French Revolution, Jefferson made him an offer. In 1803, Napoleon snapped it up right away, as he had no interest in expanding his empire across the sea. Jefferson then sent out Lewis and Clark to map the area. It included the current states of Arkansas, Kansas, Iowa, Nebraska, South Dakota, Missouri, Montana, parts of Wyoming, Colorado, North Dakota, Minnesota, New Orleans and Oklahoma.

The Slavery in the Early Colonies

From the very beginning of the colonial period, slavery was common in the New World. Farming was a labor-intensive effort. Therefore, people imported slaves, mostly from Africa, to provide free labor. The markets for cotton and tobacco – the largest farming industries – didn't pay enough to support paid labor and prices were set in such a way that a plantation couldn't survive without it. In other words, the need for slavery was built into the economic system from its onset. Slavery was practiced in Europe as well. When European countries went to war, prisoners were frequently marched off into slavery. There was no ready supply of free labor in America, so early Americans would import them, mostly from Africa. Even Christopher Columbus captured natives from the islands and sold them in the slave markets in Seville, Spain in order to finance more journeys to the New World.

People in Africa were captured, forced into the cargo holds of great ships, and brought to America to be auctioned off. So many wallowed in their own filth, becoming ill and dying in the cramped inhumane conditions of the brutal journeys across the sea. Thousands of Native Americans were also enslaved.

During the late 18th Century, abolitionists put up a strong resistance to slavery. James Oglethorpe, the founder of the colony of Georgia, forbade slavery in his colony. Vermont abolished slavery in 1777. The Quakers who colonized sectors of Pennsylvania forbade the practice on religious grounds. Between 1780 and 1804, Pennsylvania passed An Act for the Gradual Abolition of Slavery, but there was a loophole in the law. It only meant that people couldn't deal in commerce with slaves, that is, couldn't be slave traders. The importing of slaves was banned by the U.S. Congress in 1808. However, smuggling was common although most of the Northern states abolished slavery. Slaves then attempted to escape to the North, and traveled what became known as the "Underground Railroad" to the North. There was no railroad per se, but a series of paths through woods, and tunnels leading on to the properties of sympathizers who would take in the slaves, feed them and clothe them along their harried journey.

War of 1812

As early as during the administration of John Adams, the British and French were seizing ships and pressing American sailors into service during the European wars. What's more, Britain was at war with Napoleon in France, and attempted to block American merchants from trading with France, Their chief concern was weapon shipments and the provision of supplies for the French army. In 1810, James Madison who was serving as the American president at that time, blocked all trade with Great Britain. They were considered worse offenders, as they had agents in American near the Northwestern border, providing weapons for Native Americans to prevent Americans from settling the Western frontier.

Although American had emerged from the Revolution and didn't want another war, there was political pressure in Congress to go to war. In June of 1812, America declared war against England. The Federalists in Congress opposed the war, but the Democratic-Republicans favored it. In the north, where most Federalists lived, it was called "Mr. Madison's war."

The Americans lost their bid for the possession of Canada, which they had hoped would yield a grand prize for the country. That boosted the hopes of England. In 1813, America gained control of Lake Erie, one of the Great Lakes, but the British blockaded American ports, and the country languished commercially. Then the British tore through New York State burning what farmhouses they came across. Although the Americans did repel a full-scale invasion of New York and Maryland, they inflicted a lot of damage on that area. At the Battle of Baltimore in the harbor in Maryland when the British were bombarding Fort McHenry, a lawyer named Francis Scott Key was crouching on the deck of his ship. It was there that he wrote the lyrics for the *Star-Spangled Banner*, which became the country's national anthem. In 1814, the British burned Washington D.C. James Madison and his cabinet fled. It was said that James Madison's wife, Dolley had their slave, Paul Jennings, save a very famous painting of George Washington by the well-known portraiture artist, Gilbert Stuart.

At the Battle of New Orleans, General Andrew Jackson – a rather aggressive military officer – rushed to the defense of the city when it was threatened during the war. He launched a night time raid at an encampment of British redcoats. There he widened a local canal and used the displaced dirt to create an enormous earthenwork dike. The main formation of British soldiers were nearly cut to ribbons by cannon fire. The British lost about 300 men while America lost only 32. It was an astonishing victory, and saved the city of New Orleans.

Military experts indicated that the outcome of this war was a "draw," but there was no longer impressment of American sailors after it, and trade again resumed as it was before. Americans looked upon it as the "Second War of Independence," and it discouraged England from future efforts to interfere with American trade.

The Creek War

Concurrently with the War of 1812, wars with the Native American tribes continued. Davy Crockett was a hardy frontiersmen who served with the Tennessee Militia in suppressing a war with the Creek warriors. James Bowie was a member of the Texas militia. It was fought over the efforts of the U.S. government to assimilate the Native Americans and the territories they occupied, while still maintaining their nomadic cultural practices. According to the treaties, they were placed in reservations if they wished to continue their indigenous practices. The Creek Nation, however, resisted and continued to live in Georgia. It ended with the Treaty of Fort Jackson which surrendered more than 23 million acres of Creek land to the United States.

The Trail of Tears

The hero of New Orleans, Andrew Jackson, became president in 1829. After the Louisiana Purchase, Americans rushed out to settle in the new lands west of the Mississippi River to build homesteads. However, many Native American tribes populated those land, and conflicts ensued. In order to create room for both the Americans and the indigenous population, the *Indian Removal Act* was passed in 1830.

It was one of the most tragic episodes in the history of America. Tribes were given the choice of becoming citizens in the territory in which they lived, which meant they must adopt "white man's ways." Most didn't want that, as they had been raised in an entirely different culture. This would rip them from their heritage and noble history. Regardless, in the interest of peace, they were forced on marches of thousands of tribes from Alabama, Georgia, Arkansas, North Carolina, Florida and Tennessee. An estimated 60,000 of the tribes, including escaped slaves and even some white women who had been taken as spouses, left.

Tribes included the Cherokees, Creeks (Muscogees), Chickasaw and Seminoles from Florida. Many wore ragged clothes and walked barefoot during one of the coldest winters in the early records. There were physicians that accompanied them, along with their tribal leaders, but many became ill along the way and died sorry deaths on the trail. The officials attempted to keep the Whiskey merchants and gamblers from interfering with the tribes, but only had limited success. Many of the tribal people contracted cholera, smallpox, pneumonia, measles and dysentery on the journey west. The next difficulties faced by the Native Americans was the fact that the new territories were unfamiliar to them. They couldn't raise the same crops they did when they were in their homelands, and the animals they hunted were gone. It was an enormous adaptation they had to make, and many didn't survive.

Slavery Revisited: The Missouri Compromise

The issue of slavery was kept alive by the scores of abolitionists who persistently campaigned against it. As the colonies and western territories were being settled, questions arose as to whether or not these newly-formed states would allow slaves or not. In 1831, Nat Turner, an escaped slave from Southampton Country, Virginia, organized a rebellion. They didn't use firearms, for fear of the commotion it would create, but instead used axes, hatchets and knives. Turner and his men hacked and slashed with impunity and without mercy.

The Virginia militia was called upon to respond. Again bloodshed polluted the hungry dirt. About 120 slaves were slaughtered. Although the revolt was quelled in just a few days, it aroused great fear. The states executed the leaders of the rebellion, included Nat Turner in what was a shameful chapter of American history.

In 1820, an infamous piece of legislation was passed – the *Missouri Compromise*. It permitted the admission of Missouri as a slave state in exchange for the admission of Maine as a free state. Furthermore, it prohibited slavery north of 36° latitude. It banned slavery from many of the territories in the *Louisiana Purchase*, and out west. The Southern states, however, remained slave states.

Westward Ho!

During the 1800s, people raced westward to build new homesteads and towns. America passed a series of *Homestead Acts* from 1850 onward. It was an effort to settle the country, and land was initially given away by the U.S. government for free.

Hardy pioneers then packed up their belongings, furniture, tools and stuffed as much as they could inside covered wagons. Only the most courageous participated. This was raw land. People were subjected to hardships, as they had to bring their own grain and foodstuffs with them. Water was carried in massive barrels. Wagon wheels broke off on rocky ground, and they had to repair them if they could. Sometimes, parties of wild Native Americans descended upon them. These people were intruders on their hunting grounds and threatened to expand across their wide open lands. Hostility would erupt as they ushered their wagons in a circle to shoot at members of the offending tribe. Many a wagon train or idle traveler would come upon their remains. Sadness was brief, as they raided the wagons for leftover food and clothing. The tribes, too, were nomadic wanderers in unfriendly lands. The dirt of the open plains is the grave to many – both the white man and his tribal enemies.

"Cowboys" came – men clad in leather who spent days on their horses and herding thousands heads of cattle, stopped only to let them feed and water. They were brought into the meat markets for slaughter and distribution to feed the masses with rich red meat. Although the movies picture them romantically, they were, in truth, often half-nourished and lonesome. Generally, they worked for one season on long cattle drives, and spent the rest of the year spending their money, often unwisely, on whiskey and women. The more responsible among them established new ranches and founded towns.

They were later followed by "sod-busters," who were people intent upon farming. Arguments and lethal battles arose between the farmers who fenced in their land and the ranchers who preferred the open prairies to create trails for their cattle across the wide open lands.

Settlements

Towns, ranches and farms cropped up in the West and Southwest, separated by miles. Some areas were moist, and people chopped the mesquite to build crude shelters. Mesquite, best described as short trees, peppered the land. Orange sap oozed from its branches and could be used as salve or mixed with water to sooth sore throats.

The area was inflicted with unscrupulous criminals, robbers and outlaws. In a town ominously called "Tombstone" in Arizona, there is a 19th Century cemetery called "Boot Hill," so-named because men died violently, that is, "with their boots on." There is no grass on Boot Hill, just well-worn gravel, mesquites, and cactus. Many of those "cowpunchers" died in gunfights, set off by tempers exploding over something trivial, or a contest between two men who wanted to test their skills with their guns. Of the 300 or so buried there, there are some wooden markers. One such marker stands over the rock-pile grave of Les Moore with the inscription: "Here lies Lester Moore. Four slugs from a 44. No less. No more." Some were killed in error, like unlucky George Johnson: "Here lies George Johnson, hanged by mistake 1882. He was right; we was wrong, but we strung him up and now he's gone."

There are a number of "Boot Hills" across the West, not only in Tombstone, but in Deadwood, South Dakota, Dodge City, Kansas, Tilden, Texas and Virginia City, Nevada.

Chapter 7 – Wars and More

"REMEMBER THE ALAMO!" – The Annexation of Texas

The Battle of the Alamo, was just one event in the Annexation of Texas. Although the Mexican settlers of Texas were opposed to the centrist regime of Mexico and declared independence in 1824, President Santa Anna of Mexico claimed that "Texacala" was an independent country.

The Battle of the Alamo was a pivotal event in the Texas Revolution. There were only roughly two hundred American soldiers defending an old mission, the Alamo. Among them were the famous frontiersmen, Davy Crockett, James Bowie and William Travis. Crockett fought in the Creek War of 1813. James Bowie was a land speculator, a wild and adventuresome man whose rose to fame when he got into violent melees, one of which resulted in the killing of a sheriff of Louisiana. William Travis was a lawyer who made unwise investments and got himself heavily immersed in debt. He married a Mexican woman and moved to the disputed territory of Texas to escape making retribution for his debts.

At the Alamo, President Santa Anna marched in with approximately fifteen hundred men. It was a massacre. Every last one of the defenders were killed including the three famous frontiersmen. Most historians place the number of Mexican casualties between four and six hundred. Despite these losses on both sides it was far from the end.

The Mexican-American War

When people in the South, mostly Anglo-American immigrants moved westward in the early 19th Century, they traveled to this part of the Mexican province of Tlaxcala. The American presidents sought to expand America into Texacala as Americans migrated westward. The whole area was, at that time, only sparsely populated by the Mexicans.

At first, the Mexicans welcomed the Anglo-American settlers as they migrated westward into their territory. Mexico then engaged in paying off the tribal communities there – mostly the Commanches, and that had a financial impact on the government. The authorities then encouraged settlers like Moses Austin and his son, Stephen, to settle there. This started an influx of even more American colonists. When the influx of potential settlers grew substantially, the authorities became alarmed. What's more, these settlers brough slaves with them and Mexico opposed slavery. They then charged a tariff for American goods, hoping to stave off the number of settlers and closed off the western border. Nevertheless, the immigration continued illegally. Much of the area was desert, but Americans who migrated there created farmlands in areas that were fertile. They acted as they did in the rest of America – that is as independent people.

In 1834, General Antonio López de Santa Anna was by then absolute president of Mexico and led an army to suppress these single-minded people of Texas. In 1845, Stephen Austin called upon the settlers to resist and declared independence from Mexico.

The American President at the time, James K. Polk, reached out secretly to Mexico to purchase New Mexico, an unclaimed area of Texas up to the Rio Grande River, and California. The Mexican president didn't respond. The U.S. Congress was divided over declaring war, as were some of the statesmen and politicians. The warmongers won out and war was declared.

The U.S. sent its army into Mexico, and occupied Texas, New Mexico and California. A large contingent under General Winfield

Scott captured Monterey, Buena Vista, Veracruz and finally Mexico City itself.

The Mexican army was besieged by massive illnesses such as yellow fever and smallpox. These diseases were exacerbated by other illnesses resulting from poor sanitation which lead to the Mexican surrender.

The Treaty of Hidalgo of 1848

As result of the war, 525,000 square miles was added to the United States. That included the current-day states of Colorado, New Mexico, California, Arizona, Wyoming, Utah and Nevada. In addition, America paid Mexico $15 million.

Causes of the American Civil War

The slavery issue was considered the cause of the Civil War in America, but there were other issues that separated the North and the South.

The Tariff of Abominations

In 1828, Congress passed a tariff to be charged on goods imported from overseas. That was done to keep the prices of goods manufactured in America less expensive than goods imported into the states.

Up After the War of 1812, countries in Europe were charging less than the Northern states in the U.S. manufacturing companies in the North couldn't afford to cut their prices any lower because it didn't cover the costs of producing the goods.

The South, however, was basically agricultural and depended upon manufactured goods in order to function efficiently. They had mostly bought manufactured goods from overseas. Due to the tariff, they were forced to pay more for the same goods regardless of who sold them. Southern meeting houses and saloons filled up with men shouting about the injustice of the tax. That tariff favored the North while hurting the South.

Word reached Washington and the new president, Andrew Jackson, the noted military leader reacted along with Congress. They then reduced the tax in 1832, but it wasn't sufficient enough to satisfy the farmers and plantation owners especially those in South Carolina who had been especially hurt by an economic downturn during the 1820s. So, South Carolina "nullified the ruling." They simply wouldn't pay the tariffs. That was called the Nullification Crisis. It was resolved in 1933, but it left a tariff on the goods, although it was lower.

The tariff issue left a sour taste in the mouths of the Southerners, as it pointed out a preference on the part of the Federal Government toward the North.

<u>Slavery</u>

The *Missouri Compromise of 1820* did resolve some of the disagreements over slave and free states, disputes arose over the rights of people from a slave state to take their slaves into the Western territory. What's more, the Constitution passed in 1789 permitted slavery. The term "slave" was deliberately avoided by the framers of the Constitution, but some considered Article I, Section 9 as permitting slavery. It reads: "The Migration and Importation of such Persons as any of the States now existing shall think proper to admit, shall not be prohibited by the Congress prior to the year one thousand eight-hundred eight." (In 1808, the slave trade was prohibited.)

The framers of the Constitution weren't in favor of slavery. They saw it as an institution that existed at the time the Constitution was written, but felt it would eventually die out. Nevertheless, Their ambiguous wording would allow the Constitution to be open for debate and permit a change of interpretation, not a rewriting. It was written in such a way as to allow for that time in the future when slavery would be abolished.

The Compromise of 1850 was a series of bills designed to resolve the issues. It:

1. Admitted California as a free state
2. Utah and New Mexico were permitted to decide for themselves as to whether they would be slave states or free

states

3. A border would be delineated between Texas and America
4. An ancillary bill was attached to this called the *Fugitive Slave Act*. It required citizens to apprehend runaway slaves and denied them right to trial by jury
5. Permitted slavery in Washington DC

The *Kansas-Nebraska Act of 1854* effectively repealed the *Missouri Compromise of 1820*, though. By virtue of that, the Federal Government no longer maintained the free-state/slave-state balance to new states. Instead, new states were permitted to decide for themselves.

Congress discovered that the *Kansas-Nebraska Act* didn't resolve the issue at all. Violent riots occurred all over Kansas over the issue, giving that episode the term "Bleeding Kansas." It was in essence a one-state civil war between those in favor and those opposed to slavery. The members of one side were called "Border Ruffians," and those of the opposing side were called "Free Staters." Hundreds died.

The Republican Party

The Republican Party was founded in Wisconsin that same year – 1854. It stood firmly against slavery. In the 1856 Presidential election, John C. Fremont, the abolitionist, ran against James Buchanan, a Democrat, and Millard Fillmore, a Whig. The Southern states threatened that they would secede from the union (the United States) if Fremont, or any other Republican, for that matter, was elected. Buchanan won with 174 electoral votes.

"John Brown's Body Lies A-moldering in the Grave"

The original lyrics for a song named after him were written in 1861 and most frequently sung to the melody of Glory Hallelujah. "...He's gone to be a soldier in the army of our Lord; He's gone to be a soldier in the army of our Lord; He's gone to be a soldier in the army of our Lord. His soul's marching on. Glory Hally, Hallelujah! Glory Hally, Hallelujah! Glory Hally, Hallelujah! His soul's marching on!"

Some of those Free-Staters from Kansas linked up with a fiery abolitionist named John Brown. It was his intention to trigger a massive slave rebellion. On October 16, 1859, Brown led a small group of farm boys and his own three sons across a railroad bridge from Maryland into Virginia, a slave state. A train came and Brown stopped it with a few bullet shots. The conductor and a non-white porter were wounded. Then John let the train continue.

After that, the group marched into the town of Harper's Ferry, Virginia. They broke down the doors of an armory, stole the weapons, and pinned down shopkeepers and some other local men. Brown took some prisoners and rushed into a firehouse. A Virginia militia arrived at noon and Brown's men were trapped inside. Soon sn angry mob gathered and gunfire ensued. It was loud and furious. Lieutenant J. Stuart approached with a white flag, promising Brown that he and his followers' lives would be spared if they surrendered. Brown shouted back boldly, "No I prefer to die here."

A battering ram went through the door of the engine house and the soldiers rushed in shooting. Ten of Brown's men were killed on the spot. Five escaped and seven were captured. John Brown's groups killed four people and wounded nine others.

A Senate committee held the trial in closed session, fearful that is would trigger rebellions – the very occurrences Brown had hoped for. John Brown was condemned to death by hanging. After the trial, the newspapers exploded with information, editorials and many speeches in favor of abolition.

Frederick Douglass, himself an escaped slave and famous orator for the cause of racial justice said, " Until this blow was struck, the prospect for freedom was dim, shadowy and uncertain. The irrepressible conflict was one of words, votes and compromises. When John Brown stretched forth his arm the sky was cleared. The time for compromises was gone — the armed hosts of freedom stood face to face over the chasm of a broken Union — and the clash of arms was at hand."

Chapter 8 – The Civil War and its Tragic Aftermath

IN THE PRESIDENTIAL Election of 1860, the Republican, Abraham Lincoln, won against John Breckinridge, the Democrat. Seven Southern states then seceded from the union, that is, the United States. A few months later, four more states also seceded. Those states called them the "Confederate States of America" and elected Jefferson Davis as their president.

Battle of Fort Sumter

The Confederates demanded the release of all Federal installations in the Confederacy, along with its armaments and supplies. Lincoln refused. Instead, he chose to resupply Fort Sumter in South Carolina and any other Federal garrisons as needed. He had the ship *Star of the West* sent down there to take care of the fort in Charleston harbor. On April 13, 1861, as soon as the ship attempted to land, it was fired upon. One of the most tragic wars of all history had started.

Negotiations were attempted between the Confederate general, Pierre G.T. Beauregard and Major Robert Anderson, the garrison commander. Talks failed and the Confederate guns turned on Fort Sumter. There were only 80 Union soldiers there, but 500 Confederates. After gunfire blasted at the fort for several hours, Anderson surrendered, as he was so heavily outnumbered. He and his men then evacuated. The South celebrated their triumph with high hopes that this war would be short and successful.

Battle of Bull Run

On July 21, 1961, the union Army arrived from Washington D.C. under the command of General Irvin McDonnell. They boldly marched toward the capital of Virginia. Suddenly, they were confronted by General Beauregard at a creek called "Bull Run." The Union soldiers crossed the waterway toward the left flank of the Confederates. The battle raged throughout the morning, and they were doing well against the Confederate troops, having pushed them up toward Henry House Hill. Reinforcements then arrived and a counter-offensive was launched. Both sides had an equal number of men. The Southerners let out the famous "rebel yell" as they advanced and galloped full-speed toward McDonell and his men. That broke the well-ordered line of the Union soldiers, and the men chaotically charged across Bull Run.

Battle of Shiloh

On April 6, 1862, the Confederacy started moving south to capture a railway junction in Northern Mississippi. General Albert Sidney Johnston of the Confederate Army fortified the nearby town of Corinth. The Union Commander, Ulysses Grant encamped his men at a Methodist Meeting House at Shiloh. He was going to be joined by the forces of Don Carlos Buell and his brigades. Before Buell's army could arrive, Johnston attacked. Grant was surprised, but his men held the field. Johnston led his forces courageously, galloping up and down the field, moving the soldiers into the most advantageous positions. In the afternoon, when Johnston was leading a unit toward a peach orchard, a bullet pierced his knee. Assuming it was a superficial wound, he continued. However, the bullet had hit an artery and blood filled the man's boot. He nearly fainted, and was removed from his horse living for only one more hour. General Beauregard took over and they fought until nightfall. In the morning, he planned to resume.

Overnight, Buell and his troops arrived. At first light, the two armies attacked separately. Beauregard's divisions were temporarily able to drive back the Union soldiers at Water Oaks Pond nearby. However, they were reinforced by General Tuttle and later Grant moved Colonel Veatch's brigade in. Beauregard's men were low on ammunition, and he had his reserve Corps under Brigadier General John Breckinridge cover the front while he retreated. Breckinridge followed suit and Grant didn't pursue, as his men were exhausted.

With the loss of the Battle of Shiloh, the Confederates lost ground in the Mississippi Valley.

Battle of Antietam

On September 17. 1862 General E. Lee and the Army of Northern Virginia moved north to finally invade the Northern territories. By that time, so much damage had been done to all the Southern cotton plantations, that he felt it was near time they did the same to the North. He went up against General George McClellan's Army of the Potomac.

Lee began by separating his forces into two huge armies. One army was destined to move upon Boonsboro and Hagerstown in Maryland. Fortunately for the North, two Union men discovered a copy of Order # 191, which had sketches of Lee's planned actions. It gave the Union under George McClellan advance warning that Confederates were ensconced in the North Woods with their loaded muskets to shoot the Union infantry on its way toward those woods. The union soldiers to the rear then mounted their artillery pieces and aimed above the Union soldiers in the woods, to land on the Confederates lurking in wait. The air was smoky from the fire of the guns from both sides. The bloodshed was ghastly, as Confederate after Confederate fell into the mucky soil.

The Miller's cornfield was toward the South, and the Union soldiers forged their way in that direction. The Confederates under Jeb Stuart fired up their artillery and followed up with a squad of mounted soldiers. Stuart was on the Union's west. Back toward the south, Confederate Colonel Stephen Lee was on high ground near the Dunker Church – a distinct advantage. The Union, too, had an advantage of high ground, as they were just behind the North Woods on a ridge. His guns set off fires, and bodies fell from their horses engulfed in flames.

Toward the East, Union Brigadier General George Hartsuff along with Colonel William Christian exchanged gunfire with Colonel Walker's Confederate brigade. Harstuff was wounded, causing Colonel Christian to flee to the rear along with Harstuff's men. The Confederates who were still mounted proceeded forward and moved into the cornfield. The Louisiana division then joined in and forced the Union soldiers away from the cornfield and into the woods to the East. Then the Union men moved in with heavy rifles and forced the Louisiana division back.

Most of the action was taking place in the cornfield, and it seemed that neither side could progress. Then, from the west woods, the Union Brigadier General, John Gibbon and his "Iron Brigade" charged into the west side of the cornfield. They were halted by Starke's Confederate division and heavy fire ensued. That was short-lived, as the Iron Brigade descended upon them causing them to back off. Starke himself was mortally wounded. Then a gap began to show due to the many fallen Confederate soldiers strewn about the flattened cornfield.

The scene of the action them shifted toward the center of the Confederates. The Union's Colonel French moved down upon D.H. Hills Confederates successfully beating them back. The least experienced Union troops under Weber were cut down by heavy gunfire. However, another unit of raw recruits were successful in pinning back the Confederates of the Alabama Brigade near what came to be called "Bloody Lane." Despite the fact that more experienced Union solders under Colonel French were called in, they succumbed to heavy Confederate fire. In less than an hour, French's Union forces had roughly one thousand seven hundred casualties.

The Tide then turned in favor of the Union. In the Southern end of the huge battlefield, the action shifted away from Bloody Lane and to the East and Antietam Creek. The Union commander, Burnside, was instructed to divert the Confederate attention, which he so did, but lost a lot of men in the process. Georgia's Brigade had been moved to defend Rohrbach's bridge and was no longer a threat. The Confederate General, John Anderson was shot in the leg, only to lose that leg several days later. Jones of the Confederates was just left with about 3,000 men.

The Union Commander, Burnside, stormed the narrow bridge and had some men move downstream to a ford in order to cross the Antietam Creek. The banks on the ford proved to be too high, and they were unable to cross there. The Union man, Crooks, then planned to attack the bridge with his Connecticut brigade in order to clear it for another incoming brigade from Ohio. There was bluff opposite the bridge which was their goal. They were pommeled with incessant Confederate gunfire, and Connecticut withdrew with casualties. Crooks wasn't familiar with the territory so his attack was diverted and they ended upstream from the bridge.

The Union commander, Burnside, then had the bridge assaulted again, using the 2nd Maryland and the 6th New Hampshire divisions. Confederates defended the bridge well and backed off Burnside with their sharpshooters. General McClellan was furious, and had Burnside push ahead, regardless of casualties. McClellan sent messengers to Burnside ordering, "Tell him if it costs him 10,000 men, he must go now." Burnside reacted angrily, hollering, "Do you think I'm not doing the best I can to carry this bridge?"

Burnside moved his men to the west of the Creek and asked McClellan for more reinforcements. McClellan could only send in about one division, saving the rest for possible imminent attack by Robert Lee. Burnside spent the rest of the day guarding the bridge from any intruding Confederate soldiers.

Lee's assault never came. He was forced to withdraw across the Potomac by evening and returned to Virginia. At the end, losses were about even. The Union had lost about 12,400 wounded with around

2,000 dead. The Confederacy had around 10,300 wounded with 1,500 dead.

War analysts called this battle a strategic victory for the union. President Lincoln was, nevertheless, disappointed that it really wasn't an overwhelming Union victory.

The Emancipation Proclamation

In 1863, President Abraham Lincoln passed an executive order freeing the slaves. The initial section read:

> "That on the first day of January in the year of our Lord, one thousand eight hundred and sixty-three, all persons held as slaves within any State, or designated part of a State, the people whereof shall then be in rebellion against the United States shall be then, thenceforward, and forever free; and the executive government of the United States, including the military and naval authority thereof, will recognize and maintain the freedom of such persons, and will do no act or acts to repress such persons, or any of them, in any efforts they may make for their actual freedom."

Lincoln also insisted that reconstruction plans be enacted for the South after the war. In addition, he reminded the states where slavery was still legal to abolish those laws from their books.

The *Emancipation Proclamation* became the 13th Amendment of the Constitution. It was ratified quickly by a two-thirds majority vote on January 31st of that year.

The Fourteenth Amendment guaranteed citizenship to all former slaves, as well as equal rights for all citizens. That wasn't passed until 1868, after the Civil War. The Fifteenth Amendment was passed in 1870. It guaranteed black people the right to vote without any conditions based on "race, color or previous condition of servitude."

Battle of Gettysburg

General Lee decided again to attack the North. Between July 1st through July 3rd, of 1863, he moved his army our of Fredericksburg, Virginia toward Gettysburg town in Pennsylvania. It was an area full of gentle slopes, but several ridges were there – Herr's Ridge, McPherson Ridge and Seminary Ridge. Cemetery Hill lay South of the town. Commander Buford laid out defenses along those ridges in anticipation of the Confederate approaches. They approached from the West on Chambersburg Pike through the town, led under the direction of General Henry Heth and his Confederate Generals, James Archer and Joseph Davis. Union soldiers posted along the way only offered light resistance.

The Union was, in the meantime, awaiting the arrival of more troops. Colonel William Gamble's cavalry was dismounted and put up a fierce fight from their hidden positions. Even so, the Confederates had pushed the Union soldiers up to McPherson's Ridge. Finally, Major General John Reynolds arrived with his Union men and opened fire. As he was moving east of the woods in front of which he was placed, he was shot dead. The less-experienced Major General Doubleday replaced him. Fighting then continued, and the Confederate General Heth's forces were also engaged. Fighting ensued throughout the morning and into the afternoon near Chambersburg Pike. General Pettigrew joined the fight, and they were able to beat back the Union's Iron Brigade who had joined in. The Iron Brigade then reconnoitered at Seminary Ridge. General Henry Hill of the Confederates had two of his Confederate Commanders drive back the attacking Union forces.

Meanwhile, North of Chambersburg Pike, Davis was successful against the Union soldiers near a half-done railroad crossing. Davis's Confederate Brigade was confronted by the Union Commander, Brigadier General Lysander Cutler and his men. In the end Davis was repelled.

Archer's Brigade then attacked from McPherson Woods near the ridge but encountered Brigadier General Solomon Meredith's Union forces who then captured Archer himself.

Fighting continued toward the town of Gettysburg. The Union General, Major General Oliver Howard, had his line running in a semicircle around the town. However, the Union didn't have enough soldiers, so Doubleday had to call upon his reserves to help at the town.

When Union positions collapsed north and west of the town, General Howard ordered a retreat to the high ground of Cemetery hill in the center of the battlefield proper. That was the area where Major General Reynolds had been killed, so the more experienced general, Meade, sent in Major General Winfield Hancock. This boosted the morale of the Union troops who fought well and held the ground.

<u>Second Day of the Battle</u>

Union General Daniel Sickles disobeyed orders, and – instead of defending Cemetery Ridge – moved westward. He was confronted immediately by the Confederate Major General Lafayette McLaws. Sickles was then north of Emmitsburg Road near Sherfy's Peach Orchard and Devil's Den. He was originally supposed to support Hunphrey and Birney, but he wasn't there, so the other two had to spread out their Union lines much thinner than was planned. The Confederates opened fire upon them. Meade rode to Sickles to demand why he didn't follow orders. Sickles then offered to withdraw. Meade refused him.

Then Meade had to pull in from his 20,000 man reinforcements. The Confederates attacked at Devil's Den and Little Round Top hill. They then drove multiple attacks into the thinly-stretched Union defensive line. They then moved into the valley, where they were beaten back by Pennsylvania's Regiment. Sickles, in the area near Devi's Den had his leg shattered and it was later amputated. The Confederate General Robert Anderson's men attempted to take Cemetery Ridge, but were unable to do so because of Union counter-attacks. The Union forces only had a precarious hold on Little Round Top hill. Meade's chief Union engineer, Brigadier General Gouveneur Warren, sent in the N.Y. brigade to defend Little Round Top. It came just in time to repel Hood's Confederate charge.

<u>Third Day of Battle</u>

Early in the afternoon, the Confederates let out a tremendous artillery bombardment. The Army of the Potomac's Union forces paused, then hit the Confederates with eighty thunderous Union cannons let loose. As this continued, the South was running short of ammunition.

Around 3 in the afternoon, the Southerners advanced toward Cemetery Hill. General George Pickett took his cavalry and charged up toward Cemetery Ridge at top speed. Fierce fire came from the Union artillery positions there and from Little Round Top. The Union soldiers then held back from the intense barrage to deceive the Confederates into thinking they'd run out of ammunition. As Pickett drew closer, he realized his soldiers had to mount a fence, thus slowing their advance. When he least suspected it, the Union opened fire again. More Union reinforcements arrived and Pickett's charge failed.

The other Union troops were stationed to the east of the town. Jeb Stuart's Confederate troops confronted them, and the armies broke up into hand-to-hand combat. Brigadier General Judson Kilpatrick launched a cavalry attack on General Longstreet's main force. As might be predicted, he lost against the massive union force under Longstreet.

This battle was a decisive victory for the Union.

Sheridan's March to the Sea

General Tecumseh Sherman was assigned the job of finishing up the Union offensive. He took a huge force with him and they marched from Chattanooga to Atlanta, Georgia. The Confederate General John Hood, who was at Gettysburg, and his comrade Joseph Johnston attacked Sherman along his way. Both lost. On September 2, 1964, Sherman conquered Atlanta, the capital of Georgia. Hood attempted a counter-attack to pillage Sherman's supply shipment. However, he was defeated by the Union forces. Hood retreated to Nashville, and the Union forces effectively destroyed the remainder of his forces there. Sherman and his men destroyed anything they could along the way—communication depots, weapons, farmland, transport vehicles and the like following a "scorched earth" policy.

In December of 1864, Sherman reached Savannah, Georgia and the the mighty Atlantic Ocean. His march to the Sea went down in history as an overwhelming Northern victory.

Battle of Five Forks

On March 30 of 1865, Major General George Pickett confronted Major General Philip Sheridan and his Army of Northern Virginia. That area was the key to the supply lines for the South, as the railroad came in there. Pickett's Confederate soldiers were seriously undermanned and his division fought at night in the driving rain. He had 6,000 infantrymen and was joined by cavalry divisions later that night. Horses and men plodded in the deep mud, sliding and falling under fire. The Union troops under Sheridan had a reserve division at Boisseau's farm, which had been destroyed in the action. Dismounted infantrymen held back an attack of repeating rifle fire on one flank of Fitzhugh Lee's division at the Southern ford, Pickett, however, crossed the northern ford against just a small force of Union men.

On the following day, Sheridan and his men pinned down the centers and right flank of the Confederate force. Then the massive V Corps of the Union troops swept in, and the Confederates were forced to retreat. That meant that the Confederates had lost control of the vital cities of Petersburg and Richmond.

Surrender of the Confederacy

General Robert E. Lee and his troops had lost both Petersburg and Richmond. He retreated westward, planning to meet the remainder of the Confederate forces in North Carolina and the Army of Tennessee under General Joseph Johnston. However, the Union army under

General Philip Sheridan cut off his retreat. The forces met at Appomattox Court House in Appomattox County, Virginia. Lee attempted to break clear through the Union' light cavalry line, only to discover that there were two full corps behind it to back him up. He then had General James Longstreet carry a white flag of truce. Then he took an assessment of the opinions of his officers, Brigadier Generals Ranald Mackenzie and George Crooke, Major General John Gordon, and Colonel Charles Venable. Gordon then spoke for the rest when he said, "I fear I can do nothing unless I am supported by Longstreet's corps." Just three days prior to this – April 6, 1865, Longstreet had 7,700 of his men either killed, captured or wounded at Sailor's Creek and he and his men were in no condition to help.

Lee then solemnly replied to the request for assessment, "Then there is nothing left for me to do but to go and see General Grant, though I would rather die a thousand deaths." On April 9, 1865, Grant and Lee met at McLean's home to draw up the terms of surrender. Longstreet was surprised when he was greeted cordially and given a cigar.

After the Confederate President Jefferson Davis realized it was over, he fled to Georgia. The Michigan and then the Wisconsin cavalries pursued his trail from Hawkinsville near Macon to Abbeville and then to Irwindale. A skirmish occurred there. Two men were killed. At the military camp there, a Union soldier from the Wisconsin cavalry spotted an old woman, but she had on riding boots with stirrups! They stopped "her," threw off her shawl, and there was President Davis himself! Davis was taken into custody and held at the prison in Fort Monroe, Virginia for two years.

The Assassination of President Lincoln

Just days after the Civil War was over, President Lincoln and his dear wife, Mary, were attending a play called *Our American Cousin* at the Ford's Theater in Washington D.C. They were enjoying the play with their friends, Major Henry Rathbone and his fiancé, Clara Harris.

At a point in the play, when there was great laughter, a shot rang out from one of boxes. A bullet pierced the back of Lincoln's head. He slumped over. Mary screamed. The perpetrator, John Wilkes Booth, an actor, then leaped over the edge of the box, breaking his leg, and ran into the crowd below. Theater personnel rushed in, picked up President Lincoln and carried him to the house of William Peterson across the street. Doctors frantically tried to save hi to no avail.

After the assassination, Booth's co-conspirator, David Herold took Booth to a Dr. Samuel Mudd for treatment. Mudd was able to help Booth with a splint, and Booth stayed at the Mudd home for around twelve hours. Afterward, they both fled to Virginia.

Booth hated abolitionists, and Lincoln as well. Booth felt that the *Emancipation Proclamation* was wrong and bad for the South. He further resented the Union for all the destruction it had imposed on the South. Upon a request from his mother, Booth didn't serve in the Confederate Army. Instead, he spent the war in the North.

Lincoln wasn't the only intended victim. William Seward, the Secretary of State was another one. His position on the evils of slavery were clear. He has been quoted as saying, "The interest of the white races demands the emancipation of all men." Before the assassination, Booth selected a man named Lewis Thornton Powell alias Lewis Payne to kill Seward. He deceived Seward's servant, saying he was delivering some medicine for Seward who was recovering from an accident. He then forced his way into Seward's bedroom, slashed an army nurse, Sergeant George Robinson, then punched Seward's wife, after which he leaped at Seward and started stabbing him. Were is not for the metal and canvas splint he had on his jaw, Seward could have died. Seward's son, Augustus burst into the room, and Powell stabbed him, yelling, "I'm mad! I'm mad!" Powell then ran from the house, but encountered a State Department messenger whom he stabbed as well. Powell then became frantic when another co-conspirator, David Herald, had already fled. Powell then ran over to a boarding house run by a female co-conspirator, Mary Suratt, the mother of another co-conspirator.

George Atzerodt was a conspirator who had agreed to assassinate Andrew Johnson, Lincoln's vice-president. However, he changed his mind and never carried out the killing.

Booth and Herold were tracked down to a farm near the Rappahonnack River. Booth was shot in an escape attempt, and Herold was arrested. Even though Mudd didn't know any of the co-conspirators prior to the assassination, he was convicted because, for over twenty-four hours, he failed to report that he had helped Booth medically. However, he was imprisoned until 1869 when he was pardoned by the new president, Andrew Johnson. John Suratt escaped to Canada and then to Europe. He was neither apprehended nor convicted. The rest of the conspirators – David Herold, Mary Suratt, Lewis Powell and George Atzerodt were hanged on July 7 of 1865.

Reconstruction

Approximately eighteen percent of all Southern white men died in the war. Estimates vary, but it was said that about 75,000 to 100,000 were killed in battle and another 164,000 died of disease. About 194,000 were wounded and a great many had amputations. Their families were left poverty-stricken. The per capital income fell from $125 to $80 per household. The South essentially remained poor until the 20th Century. The cities of Atlanta, Cbarleston, South Carolina, Richmond, and Columbia, South Carolina were virtually destroyed. That alone affected 115,900 people. Livestock from the farms was gone, and crops were ruined. Farm implements had been destroyed; lives ruined.

The Freedman's Bureau

The Freedman's Bureau, specifically called the *Bureau of Refugees, Freedmen and Abandoned Lands* was passed in March of 1865 to help African Americans improve their condition and become productive, profit-making people. Lincoln's successor, Andrew Johnson, vetoed that bill, presenting the excuse that it would bloat the size of government. The "Radical Republicans," on the other hand, felt that extraordinary measures were necessary to insure that black people were able to exercise all their rights, as granted by *the Emancipation Proclamation*. Congress was able to override President Johnson's veto.

Reconstruction was far from adequate. However, people like General Oliver O. Howard, a Union war hero, delivered food to freedmen and poor whites in the South. In addition, the Freedman's Bureau it helped the people gain labor contracts. Education was one of its primary functions. Black people also received aid from Christian organizations which had advocated abolition. Schools for nonwhites were established on all levels. In fact, General Howard later founded Howard University that catered to the nonwhites. Congress did pass legislation the led to the *Civil Rights Act of 1866,* but States kept laws on the books that kept what were called the "Black Codes." They restricted the ability of Black Americans to earn money by providing that they acted as a cheap labor force. President Johnson turned a blind eye to the Black codes for the most part, and even vetoed the *Civil Rights Act.*

In South Carolina, those Black laws prohibited non-whites from performing any job but that of servant or farmer. Two states – South Carolina and Mississippi – required that Blacks have evidence in writing that they had jobs for the coming year. Vagrancy was forbidden. Apprenticeship laws required that they work for free, but that was true for whites as well. Employers who offered jobs for a black person at a higher wage were forbidden from doing so.

The Ku Klux Clan

Six Confederate veterans from Tennessee organized the Ku Klux Klan. The men operated in total anonymity by wearing white hoods and terrorizing the black community...but not only black people, but Jews, immigrants, leftists and Muslims.These armed bandits, mostly

Confederate veterans wandered about, descending upon the houses of new black landowners, burning their house with families inside. If they came upon a black person on the road, they killed him or her and left their bleeding bodies on the road for all to see.

A former Brigadier General, Nathan Beddord Forest, developed a "Prescript," which espoused the belief that the white man was superior to the black man. The Ku Klux Klan had a hierarchy of membership, and Nathan Forrest was its first "Grand Wizard." Despite Forrest's attempts to create organization to the Klan, most groups during the years following the war operated independently like vigilante groups.

Union Army veterans then formed their own "Anti-Ku Klux Clan" group in Alabama to put in end to the burning of black churches and the whippings of ex-Union soldiers. They were armed, and blacks also patrolled their homes to defend themselves.

As result of the promotion of the *Anti-Ku Klux Clan Act of 1871*, Benjamin Butler was instrumental in the passage of that piece of legislation which combatted attacks against the suffrage rights of black Americans.

Although the Klan did resurface in years to come, this effectively dismantled the first wave of the Ku Klux Klan.

Chapter 9 – A War, a Pause for Fun, and a Financial Plunge

IN 1914, EUROPE WAS at war. It started with the assassination of the heir to the throne of Austro-Hungary, Franz Ferdinand. Most Americans didn't know who he was. However, the international relations in Europe and Russia were delicate, bordering on hostility and hatred. The balance of power was off-kilter. To make matters worse, the Spanish Flu pandemic was raging, and even many Americans died as result.

The countries of Germany, Austria-Hungary (which was united at that time), the Ottoman Empire in Turkey, its colonies, and the country of Bulgaria formed alliances against the allied powers, including the British Empire, France, Serbia, Belgium, Japan and Montenegro on the Slavic peninsula.

The United States remained neutral although it did supply Great Britain with munitions during that time. The Atlantic Ocean was patrolled by German submarines seeking out enemy vessels. According to the co-called "cruiser law," unarmed ships could be boarded by Germans, and searched for contraband. If contraband was found, the passengers and crew were supposed to be given time to climb into lifeboats and abandon the ship, which was then captured by Germany.

As Germany boarded and captured several American merchant vessels, it obeyed that cruiser law, causing no casualties. In time that changed.

Sinking of the H.M.S. Lusitania

A warning advertisement had been placed in 50 American newspapers saying: "NOTICE: Travelers intending to embark on the Atlantic voyage are reminded that a state of war exists between Germany and her allies and Great Britain and her allies..." The advertisement appeared since April 17th of 1915. Most people who read it were concerned, but didn't let it alter their travel plans, as there hadn't been any catastrophes at sea. The passengers on the Lusitania weren't particularly concerned. After all, it was a passenger ship, not a warship. There were, however, munitions for Britain in its cargo hold. On May 1, 1954, the Lusitania steamed out of New York Harbor with 1959 passengers aboard. She was a destined for Liverpool, England.

The day of May 7th started out foggy as the vessel neared the coast of Ireland, with the sky clearing at noon. "Torpedoes coming on the starboard side!" shouted eighteen-year-old Leslie Morton, the lookout at the bow. It was now about 2 PM. Explosions erupted from the cargo hold. A few minutes later, all the cabins went dark. Within minutes, the ship listed severely to the starboard side. Frantically, the crew tried to load the scrambling passengers into lifeboats. Only the lifeboats on the port side were even available. Many passengers plunged into the sea, even as they were trying to board the lifeboats.

Eighteen minutes later, the Lusitania sank in the frigid waters of the North Atlantic. Of the 1,959 aboard only 761 survived.

Even So

Americans were reluctant to enter the war. The country had been through the Spanish American War and the Civil War in the prior century. America tended to see Germany as the aggressor because it had attacked Belgium, killed thousands of people there and occupied the country. Only a few Americans had any interest in the Slavic countries or Russia. Americans, though, were concerned about England, as many of them were of British descent. Church leaders and women were dead-set against going to war. It was against the Christian code and women didn't want to lose their husbands in war. Woodrow Wilson was re-elected to serve a second term in 1916 and ran on an anti-war platform.

Even after the sinking of the Lusitania, Wilson didn't ask Congress to declare war. He felt he was following the mandate of the American people. After all, the Lusitania was a British ship. Germany, in Wilson's estimation, must have been running low on money because there was a naval blockade of German ports in place and it was enforced by Great Britain. American banks were doing well, as they were making loans to the countries at war. American manufacturers and exporters were likewise doing well. Just to be sure the U.S. was prepared, though, Wilson initiated a ship-building program for the U.S. Navy.

Declaration of War

In April of 1917, a leaked telegram called the "Zimmermann Telegram," reached Wilson's attention. It indicated that Germany was making an agreement with Mexico to help it regain the territories lost in the Spanish-American War when the U.S. gained control of Texas and a number of conjoining states.

Wilson approached Congress with the information and – on April 6, 1917 – America declared war against Germany. It was labeled as the "war to end all wars," and a war that would ensure that democracy would not be eradicated.

The *Selective Service Act of 1917* was passed, requiring that all able-bodied men between the ages of 21 to 30 to register for a draft. That act was amended to include men until the age of 45. Black people were segregated. Only two infantry divisions consisted of black soldiers. The rest performed labor functions such as freight-handling and road-building.

World War I

American women played a crucial role in World War I. They became U.S. Army nurses who served in the military hospitals and on battlefields overseas. There were over 21,000 of them.

Bilingual women who spoke both French and English served in the Army Signal Corps under the amusing title of "Hello Girls." Only 450 were selected from the 700 who joined up.

Grace Banker, a young woman from Passaic, New Jersey along with her team members served in the office of General John "Black Jack" Pershing. She and some others were moved to Saint Mihiel in France during heavy artillery shellings. Nurses were considered civilians, rather than members of the Army. For her contribution, Banker was awarded the Distinguished Service Medal.

The U.S. Marines also used the women to serve as clerks and telephone operators, and a few others served with the U.S. Coast Guard.

The American men arrived at a rate of 10,000 per day. Their fight would be in France.

<u>The Battle of Cantigny</u>

Cantigny is located in northeastern France. The Americans of the 28th Infantry were in charge of artillery. They repulsed the German artillery bombardment for most of the day of May 28, 1918. Among the Americans there was Major Theodore Roosevelt, Jr., the eldest son of the former American president, also named Theodore. They were able to hold up a weak position in the Allied line. Of the 4,000 or so who were part of that defensive line, 318 were killed. The Allies won the battle when they were able to eliminate the German gunnery positions. Of the Germans, about 1200 were killed or wounded.

<u>Battle of Chateau-Thierry</u>

On May 31 of 1918, combined French and American troops followed a rolling barrage, and even ended up fighting behind enemy lines, as they were trying to push back the Germans who had infiltrated 40 miles into French territory near the great Castle, the Chateau. It started as a surprise attack at 4:45 in the morning. They had to provide cover for the French soldiers who were setting explosives on the bridge there to prevent German access further inland. They used heavy machine-gun bombardments, which had to be precise so as to avoid friendly fire. The Allies won the battle, and the Germans were forced to retreat.

<u>Battle of Belleau Wood</u>

This battle was part of the Spring Offensive, fought for a month in June of 1918. The Russians under the new Bolshevik government surrendered, leading to the signing of the Treaty of Brest-Litovsk, which ceded hegemony of the Baltic countries over to Germany. Russia also gave up its Caucasus area to the Ottomans and recognized the independence of Ukraine.

The Battle of Belleau was fought in the vicinity of the Marne River near Paris. It involved the U.S. 2nd Infantry and a Marine brigade who joined up with the U.S. 9th Regiment. The Marines dug shallow ditches from which they fired their rifles while in a prone position. As the Germans approached on foot with their rifles raised, the American Marines opened fire. They mowed down German after German.

An overly cautious French commander ordered the forces to retreat, but the American Major, Frederic Wise, hollered back to him, "Retreat? Hell, we just got here!" Over the next two days, Major General Bundy and his men held the front until the arrival of the 167th French Division.

The U.S. Marines then attacked the Germans on what was called "Hill 142." The French attacked at the left while the American engaged in a frontal assault in a wheat field. Many men fell due to the pommeling of German gunfire.

Following the hill attack, the Marines headed directly into the German line of fire in Belleau Woods. Hand-to-hand combat ensued in the wheat fields where many marines were slaughtered. In the end the Marines stopped the German advance toward Paris with their massive American counter-attack. Combat continued for the next two days.

The 1st Battalion under Major Hughes attacked north and into the woods. However, it ceased when the soldiers encountered heavy German machine gun fire. The Germans then employed lethal mustard gas. Although the belligerents had agreed not to use it, they violated the *Hague Convention on Land Warfare*, and used the gas anyway. The Americans had to use gas masks, which the French provided them.

When the 5th Marine united under Major Maurice Shearer came in with two more gun battalions behind him, the Germans were beaten back. This battle was called one of the most ferocious battles of the war. 1,800 Americans were killed.

<u>The Meuse-Argonne Offensive</u>

During the second phase of this offensive, which started on October 4, 1918, black soldiers, who were called "Buffalo Soldiers," served with the French divisions. They launched a series of frontal assaults. The Buffalo soldiers had customarily been doing that, much to the amazement of the French. The Argonne is a famous forest in France. This second phase, successfully broke through the German defenses in three days of heavy gunfire that enabled the rest of the soldiers behind to start clearing out the Argonne. By the end of October, the woods were entirely clear of German soldiers.

The French then moved ahead from the left and joined up with the American soldiers. They then split up into two armies. One army moved toward the Carignan-Sedan-Mezieres Railroad and subsequently took control of it. The Second Army then captured German defenses to the right and the French were able to cross the River Aisne and advance. Next the American forces moved in and captured the surrounding hills.

By then, it was November 11, 1918. The war was ended, and the Treaty of Versailles was signed.

<u>The Treaty of Versailles</u>

Signed in 1919, the Treaty of Versailles, codified the terms between the Allies and Germany. It imposed penalties for losses of territories, massive reparations and demilitarization. President Woodrow Wilson laid out Fourteen Points, which was a rather idealistic vision for a post-war world, and it outlined the needs for self-determination for the various nations that were involved.

Women's Suffrage

Throughout all these years, women had been denied the right to vote. Yet, they were no less capable of making decisions that would affect the country they lived in. Women were determined by make their voices heard and their votes count. They eventually realized they had to publicize their united desire for suffrage. After many years of demonstrations and parades of signs being carried into the streets, American women blocked city streets. Over and over again the measure to provide woman's suffrage was proposed in Congress and failed.

Besides the national and states' political affairs, finally the politicians started to take notice of issues that directly affected women's lives. Among them were education, children's health, and the prohibition of alcoholic beverages.

Alice Paul, who had been imprisoned in Great Britain for acts of civil disobedience promoting women's suffrage was well-known for her work in that field of endeavor. She returned to the United States in 1910, where she continued her work. On the day before Woodrow Wilson's inauguration, she recruited 8,000 women to march in front of the White House. A notable female labor leader, Inez Milholland, rode a white horse in the parade. Some groups wanted black women to march separately, but Alice Paul responded that they could and should march wherever they wanted to.

During June of 1917, while America was involved in World War I, Alice Paul picketed the White House. She was then incarcerated. President Wilson was opposed to women's suffrage, and many said that the picketing was "an act of disloyalty!" For want of a legitimate charge, the police indicated the arrest was made because the demonstration was "obstructing traffic." To those politicians who criticized her, she responded logically: "Those who submit to authority should have a voice in their own governments."

Wilson was severely criticized for the arrest, and with great alacrity pardoned Alice Paul. More protests were staged in the time to come, more women were arrested, and there were reports that some were brutally treated.

Finally, in 1920, the women were able to gain the necessary votes to be able to vote in American elections. The 19th Amendment was then added to the U.S. Constitution.

In 1923, the women leaders wrote the first *Equal Rights Amendment (ERA)*. It took many years before it was passed in 1972.

The "Roaring Twenties"

After World War I was over, prosperity descended upon the United States. In the 1920s, the Music industry introduced Jazz. Clubs popped up like mushrooms in all the major cities. The Art Deco period took over the furniture world, and everyone wanted their homes decorated in that style.

Entertainment blossomed, and it didn't take long before television sets were in family living rooms. Manufacturers started developing inventions that made people's lives easier, especially that of women. Mixing machines, vacuum cleaners, appliances like dishwashing machines and refrigerators quickly replaced the old-fashioned ice boxes.

Fashions of all types from the traditional to the bizarre hung in all the department store windows. Automobile ads had beautiful women sitting on the hoods.

Women entered the work force as well, though they were mostly relegated to ancillary, subservient roles, but they could function alongside men in factories. Regardless of the nature and status of their positions, women were always paid less than men.

The Great Depression

People were heavily invested in the stock market, as the prices per share grew at an enormous pace. People in the United State were buying all the wonderful products advertised after the war. In order to to compete with their neighbors, they had to take out loans which the banks were thrilled to give them. Eventually demand for the American dollar plunged and, therefore, the exchange rates increased in order to continue to adhere to the gold standard. Those Americans who could, exchanged their dollars for francs. The Federal Reserve turned a blind eye to the unregulated growth, and so did the banks.

Perhaps the financial institutions were too greedy, as they had been wallowing in the repayment of foreign and domestic loans. That, in turn, inflated the exchange rates for the American dollar and corporations turned elsewhere. Then, suddenly, in 1929, the bubble burst and the stock market crashed. Men tossed themselves off buildings, committing suicide rather than face their families with empty pockets.

Farm incomes fell drastically in the Mid-West, the "Breadbasket" of the nation, due to a drought. With those "dust-bowl" conditions, mining was decreased along with the lumber industry. There wasn't sufficient attention paid to rotation of crops, irrigation and agricultural techniques to stave off dry periods. American families became swamped in debt, the real estate market faltered. Some people were evicted for non-payment of mortgages.

As the mortgage proceeds fell, so did some of the banks who had been too overoptimistic. Everyone who had bought all those terrific new products, like refrigerators, stopped buying. Factories slowed down and lay-offs inundated the industry. That, in turn, resulted in high unemployment.

Then – to balance the budget and pay off foreign loans, – the American president at the time, Herbert Hoover, *increased* taxes! Not unpredictably, the government hit a shortfall. Hoover overlooked the people he was elected to serve. He maintained a hands-off attitude toward government when it came to the economy.

The New Deal

Franklin Delano Roosevelt took office in 1933 and was immediately faced with the dilemma of resolving the Depression.

Too late into his presidency, the prior president, Herbert Hoover, realized Federal intervention was needed. Under the latter days of his administration, two measures had just been started – the *Reconstruction Finance Corporation*, run by the Federal government. It financed large-scale financial aid programs designed to shore up banks, to provide financing for the building of railroads and other agencies. The *Tennessee Valley Authority*, which was created to provide electricity and infrastructure for rural areas in Appalachia hadn't yet been enacted and was put into motion. Roosevelt continued those measues.

Other pieces of legislation were passed under Roosevelt. They called for increased government spending and were geared up toward solving the immediate problem of poverty. *The Civilian Conservation Program* immediately put young men to work in construction, especially in rural areas which was in great need for it. The *Works Progress Administration (WPA)* and *Civilian Conservation Programs* was created to provide for the construction of roads, sidewalks, sewers and public buildings. They were designed for more local projects on the small scale. The *Public Works Administration* was created to take on large projects like the building of dams, bridges, schools, airports and hospitals. The famous Hoover Dam was built between the states of Nevada and Arizona on the Colorado River. The Grand Coulee Dam was built on the Columbia River in the state of Washington. They were all part of the *Public Works Administration* projects. Others were also built in other locales.

The United States was the only country that didn't have a program to support its elderly population. In 1935, the U.S. Congress passed the *Social Security Act* to resolve that horrendous oversight. Part of that legislation was devoted to a program of *Unemployment Insurance.* A piece of the legislation called *Aid to Dependent Children* was also passed to aid single-parent households.

<u>Suspension of the Gold Standard</u>

Roosevelt was the first to declare a "bank holiday" to prevent a run on the banks. Congress passed the *Emergency Banking Act,* giving the president control of monetary practices. He ordered that all gold coins and gold certificates in circulation be turned in and exchanged for other forms of money. It was forbidden to export gold out of the country. Cash could not be exchanged for its equivalent in gold. He further reduced the gold content of ingots and bullion to about 50%. Creditors were forbidden to demand payment in gold. He set the cost of gold to $20 per ounce, and then raised that to $35 the following year. Stock prices increased as result. The supply of gold in the Federal vaults increased by 69%.

Agricultural Revisions

Congress passed the *Agriculture Adjustment Act of 1933*, by which farms didn't hoard too much surplus. For years, there had been a neglect of healthy agricultural practices which depleted the soil and further aggravated the erosion during the era of what was called the "Dust Bowl." Huge farms grew just one crop, robbing the soil of several minerals and depriving it of the ability to regrow that crop as time went on. That act encouraged farmers to alternate the types of crops they grew in order to replenish the soil. Farmers were even paid not to grow crops in designated areas so the soil could recover.

In some areas, too much food was being produced, which lowered the value of the commodity. Corn was even being burned as fuel because it was so cheap.

There had been no regulation in the farming industry and that led to unfair business practices on the part of food processors. Licenses were required, based upon the agricultural inspectors' evaluation of fair business practices. Farm and the food processing businesses were carefully monitored by the newly-formed Agricultural Administration to curtail abuse by the unscrupulous. By 1936, more power was granted to the states as they had a better understanding of the unique needs of each state.

The shock of these changes helped, but did have harmful effects until the inequities could be balanced. Some people starved for lack of food. As the prices of grain rose, people had to reduce their hog populations. When certain crops ceased being grown, there were many unemployed farm workers.

Chapter 10 – America in World War II

WORLD WAR II, FOUGHT between 1939 and 1945, was the deadliest war in human history to date. The immediate cause for its onset was the invasion of Poland in September of 1939 by Adolf Hitler, the Nazi dictator of Germany, and his desire to essentially conquer the world. On the Pacific front, it started with Japan's invasion of the American naval base at Pearl Harbor, Hawaii in December of 1941. The United States entered the war in 1941, and took part in the Western Front from 1944 to 1945. The major Allies were Great Britain, America, China and the Soviet Union. The main Axis powers were Germany, Japan and Italy. The Axis powers allied in an agreement called the "Tripartite Pact," the primary purpose of which was territorial expansion and the destruction of the Soviet Union. The Allies wanted an end to aggression and dictatorial regimes. Further, they desired independence and democracy as a form of government. In the Pacific, Emperor Hirohito of Japan craved an empire, and he especially wanted China.

The Attack on Pearl Harbor

World War I was pegged as the "war that would end all wars," but it didn't. On a quiet Sunday morning of December 7, 1941, six Japanese aircraft carriers, two battleships, two heavy cruisers, a light cruiser, nine destroyers, eight tankers, twenty three submarines, five midget submarines and over three hundred and fifty aircraft attacked the huge U.S. Naval port of Pearl Harbor, Hawaii.

The American sailors were eating breakfast in the cramped kitchens below deck or attending church services. The explosions were massive and the skies filled up with smoke. First, torpedo bombers were in the lead and thirteen of the forty torpedoes hit the battleships, while dive bombers attacked Wheeler Field and Hickham Field where aircrafts were sitting on the ground. Ensign Joseph Taussig Jr was aboard the *SS Canada*, and raced toward the anti-aircraft gun on deck, aiming it into the sky. Four ensigns aboard the destroyer, *USS Aylwin* left the harbor to pull out to sea and turn their guns toward the sky.

Four armor-piercing bombs hit the *USS Arizona*. The great ship heaved to one side, exploded and sunk with One thousand seven hundred and seventy seven souls aboard. Five torpedoes hit the *USS Oklahoma*, and it capsized. Two bombs and seven torpedoes blew up inside the *USS West Virginia,* sinking it and killing four hundred and twenty nine people. One hundred died on the *USS California* when two bombs and seven torpedoes hit it, sinking it in minutes. The *USS Nevada* was hit by six bombs and one torpedo. Then it was beached, sixty died on that ship. Five were killed on the *USS Tennessee* when it was hit by two bombs, four died on the *USS Maryland* when two bombs hit it, and the *USS Pennsylvania* was in dry dock with two other ships. The *USS Utah* was hit by two torpedoes, killing sixty four men. Nine were killed by a bomb and debris flying off the nearby ship the *USS Cassin*. "A series of deafening explosions went off. There was one hundred and ten feet of my ship that got blown away. The number-one turret flew into the air and landed hard on the deck. A fireball – fueled with ammo and gasoline – suddenly went 800 feet into the air. It shot right through me and so many others. 70% of my body was burned. My T-shirt became engulfed in flame and scorched my torso. The hair on my head was burned away," said Donald Stratton, a survivor. Over two thousand men were killed and over a thousand wounded.

Roosevelt had aged significantly since weathering through the Great Depression. Despite his age and a creeping illness, Roosevelt declared war on Japan on the radio the following day, on December 8, 1941. "This is a day that will go down in infamy," he told the American people. On December 11th, Japan, Germany and Italy declared war on the U.S.

Up until that point, America maintained neutrality. On that day, however, the *Selective Service* program went into effect. Over 16 million men were drafted and reported to their respective bases, leaving their wives, siblings and children behind. The women had to depend upon ration tickets to buy food, as so much of it was sent overseas. Small children watched from their windows as their fathers walked down the streets of America to the railroad stations. For months, the children would ask, "When is Daddy coming home from the war?" Of the 16 million men who reported for duty, around 400,000 didn't return.

U-boats off the American Shores

The Atlantic Ocean was crawling with underwater menaces, the German U-boats. At home, the older men manned crudely built towers along the Atlantic seaboard, reporting on any suspected U-boats they sighted. Many were sighted off the coastal shores of New Jersey, North Carolina and Virginia. On February 28, 1942, a German submarine torpedoed an oil tanker, the *R.P.Restor* just miles from the beach of Manasquan, New Jersey. Oil and tar balls washed up on the beach. Earlier, that same submarine torpedoed another ship, the *USS Jacob Jones*, off the tip of New Jersey at Cape May. Like the *Restor,* it sunk. To this day, there are remnants of German submarines lurking beneath the shores off the American coast.

Up the Delaware River, at Carneys Point, the DuPont Chamber Works manufactured ammunition for the war effort. Constant patrols monitored the mouth of that river.

In the Atlantic, merchant vessels were continually attacked by German submarines most of whom were on their way to Great Britain.

In June of 1941, the U.S. was heavily engaged. The U.S. Merchant Marines often manned some of these supply ships. When a ship was stopped to permit armed Germans to search for contraband, the crew sometimes had to get not only in life boats, but on crude rafts. Men had to fold their legs into those of their companion and sit in a circle, hoping for rescue. As the waters of the Atlantic washed over their legs continually, their muscles were worn away, bones were exposed and they died in agony.

Leigh Lights, invented by the British were mounted on huge B-24 "Liberator" bombers to patrol the Atlantic. The B-24, manufactured by the Ford motor Company, was like a flying tank, mounted with bombs that could blow a submarine clear out of the water. The plane wasn't heated. It was a dangerous assignment.

Air cover was provided by British merchant aircraft carriers and later by American escort carriers. The Americans used Grumman *F4F Wildcats* and Grumman *TBF Avengers*. The Allied aircrafts protected the Bay of Biscay off the northernmost coast of France, which made it dangerous for German U-boats to operate there. The Allied defensive strategy in the Bay of Biscay was so effective that the German U-boats were attacked and destroyed shortly after leaving port.

North Africa and Italy

At the Battle of the Kasserine Pass in the Atlas Mountains of Tunisia, the US Army was nearly wiped out. When General George Patton replaced the bickering Commander, Fredendall, who exercised poor placement of his forces, the tide changed. Patton enabled the British commander, General Bernard Montgomery to push the Axis powers back, and broke their defensive network in North Africa.

The U.S, 7th Army landed on the coast of Sicily, and were supported by the 82nd Airborne division who parachuted on the island in advance of the troops. The Germans then evacuated their forces back into Italy. After the loss of Sicily, the Italian public turned against their Fascist leader, Benito Mussolini. He was dismissed by King Victor Emmanuel III of Italy. Then the Allies landed on Italy proper.

Germans arrived in Italy, and launched many counterattacks with their fierce air force, the *Luftwaffe*. Around two thousand Americans,

British and Canadians were killed. The U.S. VI Corps by that time lose three battalions to the Germans. Major Ridgway flew in with the 82nd Airborne Division and paratroopers landed infantry regiments.

Another division of paratroopers landed and the 325th Gilder Regiments landed by sea. They were able to disrupt the German lines. Casualties were significantly high for the allies. On September 16, 1943, the Duke of Wellington, Henry Wellesley was killed. On that very day, though, the German commander, von Vetinghoff reported that he couldn't neutralize the Allies there.

The Germans were occupying Naples, but an Italian rebellion forced them to evacuate. Adolf Hitler then decided that the conquest of Southern Italy was no longer of interest and ordered his forces to withdraw.

America participated in the second phase of the Western Front, which encompassed Norway, Luxembourg, Denmark, Belgium, the Netherlands, Italy, France and Germany.

In Southeast Asia, the United States, China and the British Empire and others united against the Imperial forces of Japan.

Operation Overlord

On the American home-front, more young men were recruited for the war in Europe. Many had been hastily trained with America desperate to preserve its freedom. On June 6, 1944, large number of Amphibious vessels were towed to the beaches of "Omaha" and "Utah". With their rifles in hand, they mounted the sand dunes. From within those dunes were "Widerstamdsmesters," which were resistance nests and concrete emplacements casually called "pillboxes," in the dunes protected by concrete housings. Inside those pillboxes were German soldiers with heavy weaponry pointed out the narrow openings. As the men charged up the dunes they were shot by the Germans. At Omaha beach – the worst of the landings – there were between 2,000 to 5,000 casualties.

Liberation of Belgium

In May of 1940, Hitler invaded Belgium, along with the Netherlands, and Luxembourg. They occupied those countries until the end of the war.

In September of 1944, the 1st U.S. Army under General Courtney Hodges conquered territories south of Brussels. Units were spread out through the Ardennes, a dense forest in northern Belgium. It was a long drawn out campaign that set off a chain of encounters that lasted until January of 1945.

Liberation of France

In June of 1940, the Germans invaded France and drove the British Expeditionary Force out. Then they took over Paris and held France until 1944.

In August of 1944, the U.S. 7th Army and the French First Army launched Operation Dragoon, which was initiated with the invasion of southern France. Within two weeks, that area was freed. Then the Allied forces moved up the Rhone River Valley. They had to confront the German troops in the Vosges Mountains in eastern France near its border with Germany. In the north, Field Marshal Bernard Montgomery commanded the British Army's 21st group and General Omar Bradley and General Devers of America advanced from the south. By the middle of September, the 6th U.S. Army joined up with them. The Germans were then being assaulted from both the north and the south and fell back.

In Paris, the people of the city staged a full-scale uprising against the German Military Commander, Dietrich von Choltitz. Although Hitler ordered him to fight "until the last man," he chose to surrender to the French Army. At that point in 1944, it was clear that Germany was losing the war.

The Battle of the Bulge

This was the last major German offensive in the war and took place in the Ardennes. It started during a bitterly cold winter in December of

1944, and wasn't concluded until January of 1945. Americans incurred their heaviest casualties during this battle. The German took advantage of weakly defended positions in foggy weather, sending in tanks and later, their powerful *Luftwaffe* aircraft. The Allies, though, had superior air power, but were hindered by the weather early on.

The Allies were able to delay and block German advances on the key roads in the northwest and the German force consisting of over 400 tanks were depleted, as they weren't able to replace them. The *Luftwaffe* sustained heavy losses when the weather cleared and there were numerous air attacks on the planes and on supply routes. That finalized that portion of the German campaign, as the men were deprived of rations and equipment forcing them to retreat.

The U.S. 2nd Armored Division and General Patton's 3rd Army ended the siege in the north of the country when they prevented the advance of Germany's Panzer Tank Division. Nineteen thousand Americans were killed from the 89,000 casualties suffered. There were two different casualty reports regarding the German side – which left the figure between 63,000 and 98,000.

Invasion of Germany

In March of 1945, the Ludendorf Bridge over the River Rhine was captured at the Battle of Remagen after Germany had tried to destroy it a number of times, but failed. This was a crucial bridge, as it allowed the Germans the ability to reinforce its troops. It capture was effected in mid-March. It finally collapsed, but pontoon bridges allowed the Americans to cross over into the heart of Germany with 125,000 troops, tanks, artillery and trucks.

Operation Plunder

The Platinate is an area in southern Germany. General Omar Bradley and the 3rd U.S. Army captured Mainz on March 22nd of 1945. On the following day, the U.S, 9th Army and the 21st British Army Group under Field Marshal Montgomery along with the 2nd Army under Lieutenant General Miles Dempsey crossed the Rhine River and into eastern Germany. The U.S. 18th and the 16th Airborne Corps under William Simpson, General Montgomery and Dempsey opposed the German 1st Parachute Army. It was one of the most effective German forces, but was depleted at point in war – March 27, 1945.

Battle of Nuremberg

This was a 5-day battle between the U.S, Army's 7th division and the Russian Liberation Army that started on April 16th of 1945. The Allies attacked on two fronts – the east and northeast. Although Hitler gave orders to Arthur Schoeddert, who was in charge of the artillery, to destroy the utilities, he disobeyed as he realized that the end was near.

Urban fighting took place in the city itself and it was left in ruins.

Death of Mussolini

On April 25, 1945, the Italian rebels freed up the occupied cities of Milan and Turin. They captured Mussolini and executed him. As a gruesome display of victory, they hung up his body at the Piazzale Loreto in Milan.

Hitler's Suicide

Hitler and his mistress, Eva Braun, were sequestered inside a bunker in Berlin from January of 1945. In the afternoon if April 22nd, Hitler flew into a rage when he was told his commander, Felix Steiner, disobeyed his orders to counter attack the Soviet and American troops in Berlin. By April 27th, Berlin was cut off from the rest of Germany.

Hitler flew into a tirade berating his military generals, calling them treacherous and declared that the war had been lost. Then on April 29th, he married Eva Braun. On the same day, he learned about the spectacle that accompanied the execution of Mussolini and was determined not to permit that to happen to him. He shook the hands of the German officers present. He then appointed Karl Donitz as the new president of Germany and Joseph Goebbels as its new chancellor.

On April 30th, his aide, Otto Gunsche, and Heinz Linge, his valet heard a shot. They entered his study. Hitler has shot himself in the right temple and it appeared that Eva had poisoned herself with cyanide.

Goebels committed suicide on the following day, leaving Donitz as the sole head of Germany. When Donitz ordered Generals Alfred Jodl and Field Marshal Wilhelm Keitel ordered Donitz to surrender all forces unconditionally they obeyed without issue.

The End of the War in Europe

On May 23, 1945, American Major General Rooks, speaking for Dwight Eisenhower, the Commander-in-Chief of the American forces, informed Karl Donitz that his government had been dissolved and he was under arrest.

Chapter 11 – America and the War in the Pacific

THE ATTACK ON PEARL Harbor in Hawaii triggered the involvement of America. Because Japan had also declared war on China, Chiang Kai-shek declared war against Japan. So did the British Empire, as Japan attacked Hong Kong, British Burma, the British Solomon Islands and Australia – all British crown colonies.

In 1941, not only did Japan attack Pearl Harbor and Hong Kong, but it attacked and captured a American military base in Guam, an island in the South Pacific, and Wake Island, a U.S. territory.

Philippines Campaign

In 1942, the Japanese air command bombed and captured American airfields on Luzon, the largest island in the Philippines. There were as many as 135,000 troops and 227 American aircraft there. General Douglas MacArthur, in charge of the defense there, wanted to counterattack immediately, but was ordered to go to Australia, and the remaining U.S. troops retreated to the Bataan peninsula in Luzon.

Luzon couldn't be captured until the U.S. could establish ancillary bases nearby in the Pacific. To prepare, Brigadier General William Dunckel captured the island of Mindoro in the Philippines with the assistance of U.S. 7th Fleet.

To distract the Japanese, General Dunckel sent out bombing flights over Luzon. Minesweepers were also used to clear the neighboring bays of Balayan, Tayabas and Batangas. The actual attack to recapture Luzon occurred in January of 1945. Forces consisting of 175,000 troops landed shortly afterward. The American escort carrier, the *Ommaney*

Bay, was totally destroyed by Japanese kamikaze pilots who slammed their aircrafts into targets, and dying in the process.

Aircraft from the 3rd Fleet assisted the landings. At the Lingayen Gulf in northwestern Luzon, 175,000 troops from the 6th U.S. Army disembarked. They met with a lot of resistance once they reached the Clark Air Force base. The 14th Co. then moved toward Manila. Fierce fighting went on until the end of January and the U.S. took control of that base.

An amphibious landing took place southwest of Manila. They were supported by the 11th Airborne Division. Those forces captured a bridge, but the Japanese had destroyed most of the rest of the bridges. The Japanese were entrenched all over the city. By February 11th, though, the 1th Airborne Division had the whole city encircled, and 12,000 Japanese and 3,000 Filipinos surrendered.

Battle of the Coral Sea

The Japanese planned on strengthening their position in the South Pacific by invading Port Moresby in New Guinea and Tulagi in the Solomon Islands. A joint Australian-American cruiser force went in to oppose the Japanese. On May 4th of 1942, The Japanese fleet carriers advanced on the Allied naval forces. The U.S. sunk a Japanese light carrier, but the Japanese sank a U.S. destroyer and an oiler. Both ships were damaged, along with the U.S. carriers, the *USS Lexington* and the *USS Yorktown*. The Japanese carrier, the *Shokaky* was also damaged. Both sides incurred heavy losses. Both sides claimed victory, but the Americans lost a great many of their ships in the process. The Japanese, though, lost much of their air power.

Battle of Midway

On June 4th, 1942, a force of *U.S. B-17 "Flying Fortress"* bombers flew up against the Japanese invasion force. They were unsuccessful. 108 Japanese warplanes from 4 aircraft carriers inflicted heavy damage on the U.S. base on the Midway atoll. The base was still somewhat useable, so Admiral Chuichi Nagumo staged another strike. The U.S. carriers were still operational and launched a series of air attacks.

Then U.S. torpedo bombers were launched from the U.S. carriers, *USS Enterprise* and the *USS Hornet*. Nearly all of them were shot down by Japanese Zero fighter planes. The U.S. destroyer, the *USS Hammann* and the aircraft carrier, the *USS Yorktown,* which participated in the Battle of the Coral Sea were destroyed. When the Japanese Zero fighters went for refueling, another wave of U.S. bombers took off and hit 3 Japanese carriers, the *Akagi*, the *Soryu* and *Kaga.* All four Japanese carriers were destroyed and sunk. They had been part of the force that attacked Pearl Harbor. This was a significant American victory.

The Battle of Guadalcanal

This operation was part of the larger campaign to gain control of the southeastern portion of the Pacific. The battle itself took part in two phases. The first phase was fought on November 13th of 1942 and the second phase occurred from November 14th to the 15th. Guadalcanal is a large island in the Solomon Islands, off the northeastern coast of Australia. The U.S. Marines handled this action and it included the neighboring islands of Florida and Tulagi. The objective was to defend a marine/air base – Henderson Field – at Guadalcanal. It was under construction by the Japanese, and the Americans wanted to seize it and convert it to their own use. It was also significant, as it was needed to neutralize the Japanese base in New Britain off New Guinea.

After it was constructed and repurposed by the U.S., the Japanese Army and Navy made several attempts to retake it. This time, they sent in a convoy of 7,000 troops, supported by a number of Japanese warships. The battle took place at night. Robert Leckle, a Marine, described it thus: "The star shells rose, terrible and red. Giant tracers flashed across the night in orange arches...the sea seemed a sheet of polished obsidian on which the warships seemed to have been dropped and were immobilized, centered amid concentric circles like shock waves." Two American admirals, Norman Scott of the *USS Atlanta* and Daniel Callagan of the *USS San Francisco* lost their lives in the battle.

Most of the American ships that participated in the first phase had taken damage, save for a light cruiser, the *USS Helena* and one destroyer, the *USS Fletcher* which were still combat-ready. For some unknown reason, the Japanese admiral, Hiroaki Abe, broke off the fight. At the end of the day, he hadn't fulfilled the intent of the mission – to take Henderson field – and the Japanese ground forces were unable to disembark all their men.

That allowed Henderson Field to remain active and the American planes were fit and ready. Reinforcements arrived for both the Americans and the Japanese prior the the second phase. Abe was retired from the action and Admiral Nobutake Kono assumed command.

During that engagement, there was a delay in the Japanese reinforcements. Their 8th Fleet cruisers, the *Chokai, Kinugasa, Maya* and *Suzuya*, were able to bombard Henderson Field. The U.S. launched 36 aircraft and the Japanese launched 64. Due to the fact that the Japanese had to rely on one warship to make deliveries of fresh ammo and equipment to the those who were finally able to disembark at Henderson Field, they didn't receive enough replacement supplies to sustain their forces on the island. The Americans consistently improved their strategy as the battle went from one day to the next, but the Japanese were unable to do so. In the Naval portion of that phase, the Japanese lost a battleship, a destroyer, but as many as four transports carrying Japanese troops had to be beached without much opportunity to unload equipment. The Americans lost three of twelve destroyers, and only one battleship was moderately damaged. It was a victory for the Americans.

The 1944 Presidential Election

Franklin Roosevelt won the presidential term in 1944. Harry S. Truman was his vice-president. However, Roosevelt was ill with atherosclerosis and heart disease. He confided to his advisors that he wanted to resign his presidency after the war. Therefore, Roosevelt's campaign advisors were careful in their selection of a Vice-Presidential candidate. Roosevelt was then convinced to support Harry S. Truman, a vibrant and active senator from Missouri as his running mate.

Roosevelt attended the Yalta Conference to discuss the disposition of the countries after the termination of the war in Europe. People were surprised how feeble he appeared. His physical condition was kept hidden from the American public. Roosevelt's physicians, though, sent him to his vacation home in Warm Springs, Georgia and Vice-President Truman stayed at the White House to handle state matters.

Iwo Jima

This was a major offensive was carried on between February 19th and March 26th of 1945. There were two airfields on this island, and the Americans wanted them for two purposes – to provide airstrips for damaged B-29 aircraft and to provide airstrips for the launching of fighter escort planes. It was being used as an early warning base for the Japanese to alert their mainland of any incoming Allied attacks.

This was the site of some of the fiercest battles to take place during the war. The Japanese were well entrenched on the hill there, fortified with bunkers, miles of tunnels, and hidden artillery. The Americans had the support of 110,000 Marines as ground forces, boats for an amphibious landing the backup of the Navy, escort vessels and 500 ships. The Japanese had about 21,000 troops, 23 tanks, naval guns and anti-aircraft guns in place.

However, the beaches were made up of volcanic ash, making it nearly impossible to dig foxholes. There was some defensive action on the part of the Japanese, but it was unremarkable. General Kuribayashi of the Japanese forces lay in wait until the American men and equipment were unloaded on the beach. Without warning, machine gunfire ripped through the air and into the ground forces. Mortars and heavy artillery shells rained down upon the unprotected soldiers. Even the concussive reaction of the intense noise knocked men down before they could fire. Landmines were planted everywhere. American bulldozers were finally able to plow roads for the movement of men and equipment, but with a great loss of life in the process.

However, the Japanese there were heavily outnumbered. 30,000 Marines were followed up by 40,000 more. Even so, they fought courageously, reoccupying open bunkers that had been cleared with American flamethrowers.

Then they were assaulted with night time attacks and had to engage in hand-to-hand combat. Once landing areas were secured, even more American equipment came in. While this was going on, airplanes flew over with lights during the nighttime raids.

The Japanese would hide and then jump out at a soldier just as he was approaching. Little by little, the Americans climbed Mount Suribchi on the southern end, and then had to attack the Japanese who heavily fortified the north. A photo of the planting of the U.S. flag on that mountain became a classic.

Out at sea, a kamikaze fighter attacked the *USS Bismarck Sea*, sinking it, and damaging the *USS Saratoga*. As the battle reached its eighth day, the Japanese in their bunkers ran out of food. Once the battle reached its end, the American dead outnumbered those of the Japanese.

Battle of Okinawa

This battle was fought between March 26th and July 2nd of 1945. This, too, was one of the bloodiest battles in the war. As this huge island was south of Japan itself, the Americans planned on using an air force base there in order to attack the Japanese mainland. The Marines and tactical air force unit, the 10th Army, worked in conjunction with 4 U.S. Army infantry units and 3 divisions of Marines. America was supported by troops from the United Kingdom, Canada, New Zealand and Australia.

There were 82 days of brutal warfare on Sugar Loaf Hill and Kunishi Ridge. Many civilians were killed – native Okinawans. Some were fighting with the Japanese troops, but most were caught in the crossfire. Between 40,000 to 100,000 of them died. Many, many committed suicide, as they had been told that the Americans would torture them, or perform untold cruelties upon them. That wasn't true but the propaganda had its deadly effect. In some cases, the Americans actually did shoot inside Okinawan homes in search of enemies hiding there, as they became so detached after so many days of fighting.

Of the Japanese commanders of their ships, 4 out of 5 were killed or chose to go down with their ships. One was taken as a prisoner of war. One American Lieutenant general and a brigadier general were killed. With 14,000 to 20,000 Allied soldiers killed and 77,000 Japanese dying there, this was a distinctive Allied victory.

President Roosevelt was worn out from the strain of carrying America through the war in Europe and was still struggling to end America's campaign in the Pacific theater. Weary and exhausted Roosevelt went to his vacation home in Warm Springs, Georgia until the war could be concluded.

Chapter 12 – Postwar America

WARS KILL MORE THAN Soldiers

Following World War II, President Roosevelt was worn out from the strain of carrying America through the war in Europe and the Pacific. He was sent to his vacation home in Warm Springs, Georgia to rest. They had him sit for a portrait and as he sat in chair, he wearily looked up and muttered to the artist, "I have a terrific headache." Then he slumped forward. Within hours, he was dead. The date was April 12, 1945.

Mrs. Eleanor Roosevelt walked up to Vice-president Harry S. Truman and informed him. "Is there anything I can do for you?" he asked.

"Is there anything we can do for you?" she asked in reply... *"For you are the one in trouble now!"*

Vice-President Harry S. Truman was then sworn in as the new President.

Atomic Bombs

For the first time in history – August 6, 1945 – America dropped an atomic bomb on Hiroshima. After President Harry S. Truman demanded that Emperor Hirohito surrender, he failed to do so. Then, on August 9, 1945, the U.S. dropped another atomic bomb, this time on the city of Nagasaki. The emperor then surrendered with more than 129,000 people dying as a result.

Crisis Time

Eleanor Roosevelt's ominous statement to Harry Truman – "You are the one in trouble now" – was correct. Truman *was* in trouble. So much money was poured into the war, that America was in financial straits. Prices had been deliberately kept low during the war. Suddenly, they skyrocketed up so that companies could make up for their deficit. Workers couldn't earn enough money to buy products, so a national railroad strike hit the country. Railways were the single means of public transportation, meaning the country was virtually immobilized.

Truman was a person who never minced his words. He was furious and fired back, "Every one of the strikers and their demagogue leaders have been living in luxury...Let's put transportation and production back to work, hang a few traitors and make our country safe for democracy!"

The Berlin Airlift

After World War II, the Allies met at Yalta in Ukraine and Pottsdam in Germany in 1945 to discuss the disposition of Germany. They divided the city of Berlin into occupied zones with the intention of reuniting the city. The Eastern portion was under the control of the Soviet Union and the western sector was controlled by the other Allies. The Soviet Union intensely disliked the fact that East Berlin was a capitalist city as Russia was communist. Therefore, they wanted to prevent the unification of Berlin as the capital of Germany. Berlin was only around 100 miles from their border. In June of 1948, the Soviets closed the Autobahn, the highway connecting West Germany and Berlin. All rail traffic into the city was likewise closed. Without warning, all the people living in Berlin had no fuel, food or supplies. To resolve the crisis, the Allies then airlifted food and supplies to the people. The world considered this to be a temporary situation, but it went on until 1949.

The "Red Scare," McCarthyism and the Cold War

After World War II and the defeat of Germany, there were essentially two superpowers left in the war – America and the Soviet Union. Politically, they were diametrically opposed ideologically. Capitalism was practiced in the United States and other countries.

Capitalism is an economic system by which trade and industry are under the control of private entities rather than by the state. In the Soviet Union with its communism, the opposite was true.

In 1949, the Soviet Union successfully tested its first nuclear bomb. This propelled a condition called "Mutually Assured Destruction," ("M.A.D.") which means that if two parties have weapons that can annihilate each other, it might serve as a deterrent against war between them.

In America, people had a mortal fear that Communism would infiltrate their country. On March 21st of 1947, in fact, President Truman passed *Executive Order # 9835*, requiring that all Federal employees take an oath of loyalty. He also promoted what became labeled the "Truman Doctrine." That quickly became the foundation of American foreign policy. Truman stated to Congress "It must be the policy of the United States to support free peoples who are resisting attempted subjucation by armed minorities or by outside pressures."

An overly ambitious senator, Joseph McCarthy started a political "reign of terror." He was paranoid and obsessively bent upon eliminating people who were suspected of having Communist tendencies. Neighbor suspected neighbor. Famous celebrities had their reputations ruined and many lost their careers. In essence, it applied to anyone who disagreed with him.

Democracy permits the formation of political parties to run on platforms of their own choosing. In fact, in America, the American Communist Party often runs its own candidates in presidential elections. Communists were called the "Reds," a reference to the flag of the Soviet Union, that has a hammer and sickle pictured against a red background.

The Red Scare fever spread to J. Edgar Hoover, the Director of the F.B.I. He was a fervent anti-communist. He often targeted people who disagreed with him politically. Hoover resorted to underhanded means like unapproved wiretaps and even the planting of forged documents in the homes of people he planned to victimize.

One could even speculate that the Red Scare that prevailed at the time wasn't dissimilar to the kind of thinking that motivated the Salem witch trials, except for the fact it was more cosmetic.

Eisenhower to the Rescue

In 1953, the former Commander-in-Chief of the American forces during World War II was elected president. People were reacting to the fears that inundated the country following the war. However, he was a man who knew the horrors of war first-hand and felt that the country needed a respite from the paranoia of the years that preceded him. He avoided America's involvement in foreign wars during his presidency. Although he was anti-Communist, he put a halt to the rampant madness triggered by politicians such as McCarthy and Hoover.

Because he knew the proper way to prioritize values and needs, Eisenhower presided over an era of economic recovery and growth. More attention was focused upon the welfare of those who needed government programs. Governmental expenditures included housing, welfare and education. That trend continued with the election of Lyndon B. Johnson who once said "Guns and bombs, rockets and warships, are all symbols of human failure."

Again the "Red Scare" erupted with American involvement in the Vietnam War. So, too, the countries of Australia, New Zealand, the Philippines, South Korea, Cambodia and Thailand. Their political ideologies were completely opposed to communism, to Vietnam, Laos, the Khmer Republic and South Vietnam were also involved. Other countries were also engaged, but for other related purposes. Cambodia was involved, as the war in Vietnam spread to portions of their territory. Other countries joined the coalition but for varying reasons. It was triggered by the invasion of South Vietnam, a democratic republic, by North Vietnam, a communist entity. This war was a prolonged and costly one – nearly twenty years long, from 1955 to 1975. In actuality, it was a proxy war fought between the Soviet Union and the United States. One might, therefore, speculate that it was a by-product of the policy of "Mutually Assured Destruction." Deaths of both civilians and troops were very high. All totalled, between one to four million people lost their lives, of which 58,000 were Americans. In the end, North Vietnam won, and was joined with South Vietnam. Together, they became what was called the "Socialistic Republic of Vietnam." One of the most tragic effects of this war, besides the massive numbers of dead, were the unintended effects of the use of the defoliant, "Agent Orange." It not only caused severe environmental consequences, but 400,000 died because of the side effects of that powerful chemical agent.

THE CIVIL RIGHTS MOVEMENT

The Civil War of the 19th Century left behind it a tragic legacy that reared its ugly head even through the 1950s, and elements of it remain today. Segregation was practiced everywhere. African Americans were relegated to second-class seating in buses, restaurants and schools. There were even churches that were specifically devoted to serving the African-American community like the 2nd Baptist Churches. (as opposed to the First Baptist churches). In March of 1955, Montgomery, Alabama, a black woman by the name of Rosa Parks refused to seat herself in the 'colored" section of a bus. As result of that, she was fired from her job as a seamstress and received death threats for years to come. In 1960, a six-year-old girl, Ruby Ridges was escorted by four Federal marshals into William Frantz Elementary School in New Orleans, Louisiana. Up to that that day, only white children attended first grade. Of Ruby Ridges, the Deputy Marshal, Charles Burks, said "She showed a lot of courage. She never cried. She didn't whimper.

She just marched along like a little soldier, and we're all very proud of her." There were protests outside the school, but they subsided as other parents brought their children to the school.

Regardless, her father lost his job as a gas station attendant, and the grocery store at which the parents shopped ceased waiting on them.

School integration was gradually introduced in America during the 1960s and 1970s.

Race Riots

It was a long, hot summer in 1967. In the primarily African-American City of Newark, New Jersey, a white mayor, Hugh Addonizio, waved from his black Lincoln at the end of the Thanksgiving Day Parade. As the parade turned on to street in the north side of the city, a predominately white area, no one waved back. The people of the city knew what he stood for. His supporters had, for years, been paying him to secure city employment and construction contracts for themselves. He was reported as stealing as much as $1.5 million in such funds, and was finally sent to prison for ten years. Such illegal practices went on in major cities in America for years to come, and was the result of discrimination against the African-American community and black politicians who ran for office.

In the cities of Newark and Plainfield New Jersey and Los Angeles, California, race riots broke out. Store windows were smashed cars set afire, and gunshots rang out in the central city areas. These would happen suddenly, causing businessmen and workers to hide in the back of stores or climb under their vehicles to protect themselves. Looting was widespread. Even young white men left their homes at night to "go looting." Appliances such as televisions, washing machines and clothing were carried away. Some civilians were killed and many wounded when law enforcement stepped in to control them. In Los Angeles, an officer was shot in the process. In the end, the riots resulted in $10 million in damages. Today, Newark is peppered with abandoned buildings and empty lots. The mayor reports that there is an insufficient tax base to support the city and it is still one of the poorest cities in the country.

Civil Rights Leaders

The Civil War saw a racial divide, but the issue wasn't entirely resolved with the passing of the *Emancipation Proclamation in 1863.* It was an on-going struggle to bring about equal treatment of both African-Americans and other Americans.

Martin Luther King, Jr. was the most noted of all the Civil Rights leaders. He experienced racial prejudice due to the segregation of black people and white people. It inspired him to donate his life to bringing about justice for all people. He believed that resistance was the most effective way to bring about that transformation. In 1964, he was awarded the Nobel Prize for his untiring efforts in that regard.

In 1965, he led a five-day march from Selma to Montgomery, Alabama to demonstrate against racism. King uttered the most quoted line of the appeal for racial justice when he said, "I have a dream that my four little children will one day live in a nation where they will not be judged by the color of their skin, but by the content of their character." On April 4, 1968 , he was assassinated by a racist belligerent, James Earl Ray. Among other Black Civil Rights leaders were John Lewis, congressman, Malcom X, Stokely Carmichael and Jesse Jackson.

Women's Liberation Movement

Back in the 1950s, television commercials pictured women cooking and cleaning. Little musical jingles blasted out within homes, while the visuals showed women cheerily cleaning and cooking with modernized products for making the work easier and more efficient. They happily cared for their children and awaited the arrivals of their husbands from work.

With advent of the 1960s, the American economy shifted, making it not only necessary but more fulfilling for women to participate in the work force. Discrimination then set in when the business community started paying the women less for the same amount of work that men did. There were gender-related differences that arose due to unequal treatment. Those attitudes, in part, sprung from the traditional belief that men are "supposed" to support their wives and families. Women protested. There were marches and demonstrations across America to achieve equal rights for women. To respond, the Federal Government passed a number of laws aimed at meeting these new needs regarding employment, education and gender discrimination. Supreme Court rulings surrounding the 14th Amendment were directed toward helping women attain equal status. It is still an issue today.

9/11: The War on Terror

On September 11, 2001, the United States was hit by a terrorist attack on the tallest building in the country – the World Trade Center. Nearly 3,000 people died as result of that attack. It had been motivated by an Arab extremist group called *Al Qaeda*.

Near Shanksville, Pennsylvania the passengers aboard the United Airlines Flight 93 died in their successful effort to stop the flight which was intended to crash into the Pentagon in Washington, D.C. Like the attack on the World Trade Center, it was planned by *Al Qaeda*.

$750 million was spent on the clean-up of the site. As result of those attacks, a new department was created in the government – the Department of Homeland Security.

Conclusion

AMERICA HAS WEATHERED through its wars, some of which were caused by its own failures in promoting ineffective policies that were doomed. Some, however, like World War I and World War II, were effective in preserving the freedoms America cherished.

It was America, and not the Soviet Union, that unleashed the greatest weapon of mass destruction in the known world. Besides the horrendous loss of human life, it opened a chapter in human history that all humanity wants to avoid, irrespective of governments, ideologies and geo-politics.

As with other countries, America wasn't different in that it experienced times of hunger, disease and economic depressions. People lived and died, sometimes for a good cause, and sometimes when they didn't need to die. For any failings it might have it still stands as the land of the free and home of the brave. The basis for its existence is democracy in a world where so much pain exists. Has it made mistakes? Like all countries the answer must be yes but what is more important is its people. When something isn't right the people have a voice that allows them to enact change.

Afterword

Thank you for reading this concise history of America. Our goal is to make history informative and enjoyable without blocking up our books with filler. If you have enjoyed this book please leave a rating or review, it allows us to reinvest and bring you more History Nerds content.

You can also visit our website below and sign up for our newsletter where we include offers and news of new releases.

https://historynerds.mailchimpsites.com

Don't miss out!

Visit the website below and you can sign up to receive emails whenever History Nerds publishes a new book. There's no charge and no obligation.

https://books2read.com/r/B-A-ODOK-RYFLB

BOOKS 2 READ

Connecting independent readers to independent writers.

Also by History Nerds

Celtic History
Ireland

Great Wars of the World
World War 1
World War 2
The Napoleonic Wars: One Shot at Glory
The Serbian Revolution: 1804-1835
Peace Won by the Saber: The Crimean War, 1853-1856
The Wars of the Roses

Irish Heroes
Grace O'Malley: The Pirate Queen of Ireland
William Butler Yeats: Nobel Prize Winning Poet
Scáthach
Finn McCool

The History of the Vikings

Vikings
Longships on Restless Seas

The Rise and Fall of Empires
Rome: The Rise and Fall

Standalone
The History of the United Kingdom
The History of Ireland
The History of America
Stalin
The Fiery Maelstrom of Freedom
The History of Scotland
Robert the Bruce
William Wallace: Scotland's Great Freedom Fighter
The History of Wales

www.ingramcontent.com/pod-product-compliance
Lightning Source LLC
Chambersburg PA
CBHW031742150726
47989CB00006B/2567